CONTENTS

	Preface	v
I.	The Paragraph	1
II.	The Topic Sentence	7
III.	The Rest of the Paragraph	17
IV.	Writing Your Own Paragraphs	25
	A. Methods of Paragraph Development	25
	B. Finding Ideas	39
V.	The Characteristics of a Good Paragraph	50
	A. Unity and Consistency	50
	B. Order	53
	C. Coherence	55
	Paragraph Checklist	64
VI.	From the Paragraph to the Whole Essay	65
	A. The Structure of the Essay	65
	B. Connections between Paragraphs	71
	C. For Further Thought	82
	Example of a Mind Map	87
	A Brief Guide to American Punctuation	88

Preface

Learning how to write well-organized paragraphs and essays in English is an essential step in a university education, and for generations of students at Tsuda University, *Effective Writing: From the Paragraph Up* has been the point of departure on their paths to writing proficiency. It has done this by introducing students to key concepts such as *topic sentence* and *paragraph development*, to a rich abundance of example paragraphs, and to exercises that challenge students to analyze paragraphs, improve them, and use them as models for new paragraphs of their own.

Effective Writing started out as an in-house publication exclusively designed for Tsuda students. A faculty member called Masako Nakanishi produced the first edition in the 1960s, and it has been used in Tsuda's writing program ever since. Other faculty members have contributed to the textbook since then, notably Mary Althaus and Akiko Ueda—between 1995 and 1999—with their revisions of the book's explanatory text, their new example paragraphs, and their additions of a teacher's manual and a punctuation appendix. Around the turn of the century, *Effective Writing* came out in print and became available to a wider audience of students and teachers. The current New Revised Edition is an updated version of the Revised Edition that was prepared by Mary Althaus and published in 2001.

The need for a new edition of *Effective Writing* is mainly due to historical developments. The world has changed in numerous ways since 2001, and many of the book's example paragraphs have become outdated in the process. It made sense to have paragraphs about VCRs (videocassette recorders) and CDs (compact discs) in 2001, because in those days, these were technologies that students used all the time in daily life. Students today may have heard of VCRs and CDs, but for watching videos or listening to music, they are more likely to use streaming services. In reflection of changes like these, new paragraphs (including a paragraph about streaming music) have been added to replace outdated ones from the previous edition.

Another historical change is related to the growing recognition that language use should be non-sexist and inclusive. Pronouns such as *he* and *she* illustrate the need for this recognition very well. In the past, the pronoun *he* could be used to refer to men and women so that "he" in the following example would have been understood to refer to male and female students: "When a student enters university, he will want to make new friends." This is the so-called "generic *he*," and in the second half of the twentieth century, it became widely recognized that it was sexist. To avoid this kind of sexism, the 2001 edition of *Effective Writing* used a system of alternating equally between *he* and *she*, sometimes writing *a student . . . she* and sometimes *a student . . . he*, for example.

Nowadays, being aware of the need to avoid sexism in language remains important, but the need for inclusiveness has gained more and more attention. Not everyone wishes to identify as *he* or *she*, and in recognition of this, it is sometimes preferable to use plural forms such as *they*. This is the approach that has mainly been used in this 2024 edition of *Effective Writing* so that, for example, *the writer . . . she* or *the reader . . . he* have become *writers . . . they* and *readers . . . they* respectively. We hope that with these and other changes to the wording, we have managed to make this new edition of *Effective Writing* an inclusive textbook for all the readers and writers who will be using it.

While various revisions have been made, *Effective Writing* remains unchanged in a number of fundamental ways. The reader-friendly, interactive style of writing is one fundamental feature that remains the same. From the first chapter to the last, readers are addressed directly with questions asking for their opinions about something, with suggestions such as "Let's look at an example," and with the personal pronoun *you*. The final chapter ends with the familiar phrase "Good luck!" to wish readers success on their continuing journey towards becoming good writers of English.

The basic structure of the book is also the same as it was in the 2001 edition. The book begins with an introduction to the standard layout of an English paragraph in chapter I. The next two chapters cover how paragraphs are organized, with a discussion of their topic sentences in chapter II and of their supporting sentences in chapter III. Chapter IV introduces ten common paragraph patterns such as paragraphs that describe examples or paragraphs that explain problems and suggest solutions to these problems. Chapter V is the book's most theoretical chapter with its focus on abstract qualities of a good paragraph such as unity, consistency, and order. Finally, in chapter VI, there is an introduction to the writing of essays and how to combine paragraphs into a standard English essay.

The example essays used in chapter VI of the 2001 edition have also been retained in this 2024 edition, with minor revisions in a number of cases. Former second- and third-year students at Tsuda contributed these example essays to *Effective Writing*, and we continue to be grateful to these students for giving permission to use their writing. Their essays demonstrate to first-year students what they can hope to achieve if they make the required effort.

The team members charged by Tsuda's Department of English with the responsibility of revising *Effective Writing* for this 2024 edition are listed at the bottom of this preface. We also need to thank our colleagues Keiko Noguchi, Yasuko Suga, and Mori Nakatani for being kind enough to serve as guinea pigs by trying out our draft materials in their 2023 composition classes for first-year students and for giving us greatly appreciated feedback based on their experiences.

A few months after we started work on this revision of *Effective Writing*, generative AI was turned loose on the world, bringing tremendous opportunities for users in its wake. It even has the ability to produce creditable essays in English on demand. It is not yet possible to predict how this will affect writing instruction from now on. However, we hope that *Effective Writing* will help our students to discover that they do not need generative AI to find their own voices as writers and that the writing process itself can help learners to develop their creativity, their expressive capacity, and their critical thinking ability.

The Department of English
Tsuda University

Tokyo
October 2024

Revision team members

Jonathan D. Picken   Elizabeth I. Dow
(writing, reviewing, and proofreading)

Yoko Abe
(reviewing and proofreading, teacher's manual revision)

Yoshinori Inagaki   Hajime Ono
(reviewing and proofreading)

I. The Paragraph

What is a paragraph? **A paragraph** is a group of related sentences whose purpose is to express one basic idea. A paragraph is also normally one of a series of paragraphs (like the paragraphs on this page and in this chapter) which work together to express a broader, more complicated idea.

However, a single paragraph can stand alone and be complete in itself. Because it is short and makes use of most of the key principles of English composition, the single paragraph is a very good type of writing for beginners to practice. Students who have mastered the concept of paragraph writing will find it relatively easy to move on to writing longer compositions that are made up of multiple paragraphs.

There are two important points for beginners to remember about English paragraphs. The first is their shape. The first word of the first line of a paragraph begins a little to the right of the beginning of the second line. This extra space is called **an indentation**. It shows clearly where a new paragraph begins.

The other crucial point to remember about paragraphs has already been mentioned above—that the sentences in them are connected by a closeness of purpose and idea. All the sentences in a paragraph should work together to build up one central idea. They should work together to help readers understand that idea. They should work together to persuade readers of the truth of that idea. When writers think that they have done enough to make their readers understand and accept their ideas, they will feel that their paragraphs are complete.

Now, let's think once more about shape. A paragraph looks like this:

> Xxxxxxx xxxxxxxxxx xxxxxxxxxxxx xxxx xxxx xxxxxxxxx xxxxxxxx xxxxxxx xxxxxxxx xxxxxxx. Xxx xxxxxxx xxxxxxxxxxxxxx xxxxxxxxxxxxxx xxxxxxxxxxxxx xxxx xxxxxxx. Xxxxxxxxxx xxxx xxxxx xxxxx xxxxx xxxxxxxxxx xxxxxxxxxx? Xxxx xxxxxxxxxx xxxxxxxx xxxxxxxxxxxx xxxx xxxxxxx xxxxxxxxxxxx xxxxx.

It does *not* look like this:

> Xxxxxxxx xxxxxxx xxxxxxxx xxxxxxxx xxxxxxxxxxxx xxxxxxxx xxxxxxx xxxxx xxxxxxxxxx xxxxxxxx.
>
> Xxxxxxx xxxxxxxxxxxxxxxxxx xxxxx xxxxxxx xxxxxxxx xxxxx.
>
> Xxx xxxxxxxx xxxxxxxx xxxxxxxxxxxxx xxxxx xxxxxxxxx xxxxxxx xxxxx?
>
> Xxxx xxxxxxx xxxxxxxxxxxxxxx xxxxxx xxxxxxxxxx xxxxxxxx xxx xxxxxxxxx.

(Actually, the shape of this group of lines makes it look like four paragraphs!)

It does not look like this, either:

I. The Paragraph

Xxxx xxxxxxx xxxxxxxxxxx xxxx xxxxxxxxxxxx xxxxxxxxxx xxxxx xxxxx xxxxxx.
Xxxx xxxxxx xxxxxxxxx xxxxx xxxx xxx.
Xxxxxxxxxxx xxx xxxxxxxxx xxxxxxx xxxx xxxxxxxxxx xxxxxx xxxxxxxx xxxx xxxxxxxxx xxxxxxx?
Xxx xxxxxxx xxxxxxxxx xxxxx xxxxxxxxx xxxxxxxxx xxxx.

A paragraph looks like this:

> I am a pretty active person, so in my free time, I like to go out and do things. I love marine sports, and because my family lives near the sea, I often go surfing early in the morning with my older sister. In the summer, we also like to go snorkeling together. I enjoy swimming too, but I have not joined the swimming club at my high school because I do not want to practice for competitions all the time. Some of my friends and I want to start a surfing club at our school, but we are not sure if the school will support us. One of our teachers often goes surfing, so we are going to ask her if she can help us.

Not like this:

> I am a pretty active person, so in my free time, I like to go out and do things.
>
> I love marine sports, and because my family lives near the sea, I often go surfing early in the morning with my older sister.
>
> In the summer, we also like to go snorkeling together.
>
> I enjoy swimming too, but I have not joined the swimming club at my high school because I do not want to practice for competitions all the time.

> Some of my friends and I want to start a surfing club at our school, but we are not sure if the school will support us.
> One of our teachers often goes surfing, so we are going to ask her if she can help us.

Not like this, either:

> I am a pretty active person, so in my free time, I like to go out and do things.
> I love marine sports, and because my family lives near the sea, I often go surfing early in the morning with my older sister.
> In the summer, we also like to go snorkeling together.
> I enjoy swimming too, but I have not joined the swimming club at my high school because I do not want to practice for competitions all the time.
> Some of my friends and I want to start a surfing club at our school, but we are not sure if the school will support us.
> One of our teachers often goes surfing, so we are going to ask her if she can help us.

How long should a paragraph be?

Well, that depends. The length of a paragraph varies according to the place where it appears, its purpose, and the difficulty of the main idea. In a newspaper, for example, most paragraphs contain only one sentence. In narrow newspaper columns, however, such paragraphs will still be four or five lines long, and so they do not *look* too short. In general, difficult ideas written for highly educated readers tend to be in long paragraphs, and easy material written for beginners tends to be presented in short paragraphs.

For the time being, you only need to think about making your paragraphs long enough to express one basic idea well. Since you will need one sentence to state your main idea and several sentences more to explain it, the paragraphs you write for a class at this level should probably be about five or six sentences long.

EXERCISE 1. Look at pp. 1–4 again. How many indentations can you find (not including the examples)?

EXERCISE 2. On p. 4 there is one paragraph which contains only one sentence. Can you find it? Could this sentence have been put in the paragraph that comes after it? Which way do you like better? Why?

EXERCISE 3. Read the following long paragraph and answer the questions about it:

> There are two important points to remember about English paragraphs. The first is their shape. The first word of the first line of a paragraph begins a little to the right of the beginning of the second line. This extra space is called an indentation. It shows clearly where a new paragraph begins. The shape of the paragraph is also affected by the number of sentences in it. Most paragraphs written by good writers contain five, six, or more sentences; therefore, they are usually at least eight lines long. The other thing you should not forget about a paragraph is that the sentences in it are connected by more than shape—they are also connected by a closeness of purpose and idea. All the sentences in a paragraph should work together to build up one central idea. They should

work together to help readers understand that idea. They should work together to persuade readers of the truth of that idea. When writers think that they have done enough to make their readers understand and accept their ideas, they will feel that their paragraphs are complete.

a. Would it be possible to divide this paragraph into two shorter paragraphs? If your answer is yes, where would you divide it?

b. Think of reasons why using one paragraph would be better. Next, think of the advantages of using two paragraphs.

c. Would it be possible to divide it into three or more paragraphs? Why, or why not?

EXERCISE 4. <*Suggested Writing*> Let's get started! Choose one of the following topics and see if you can write a paragraph about it.

a. How you like to spend your free time
b. A person whom you admire, and why you admire this person
c. One ancestor whom you are interested in

II. The Topic Sentence

The sentence that expresses the basic, controlling idea of the paragraph is called **the topic sentence**. The topic sentence contains the topic and the idea about the topic that is explained in the rest of the paragraph. Another way to say this is to say that the topic sentence makes **an assertion** (a claim or forceful statement) about the topic, and the rest of the paragraph then explains that assertion. Here is a simple example:

> Mary + is a fine photographer.
> (topic) + (assertion about the topic) = topic sentence

In the rest of the paragraph, the writer will give concrete details or specific examples to show why Mary is a fine photographer. If the writer does this well, then most readers will probably understand the claim that Mary is a fine photographer.

The topic sentence often comes at the beginning of the paragraph, and that is usually the best place for it, but it may also appear at the end, or even in the middle of the paragraph. Here are two sample paragraphs in which the topic sentences have been underlined for you.

(1) It was a marvelous day. The sky was pure blue, without a single cloud in sight. The air smelled fresh and clean. The sun was warm and gentle. It no longer glared down on us as it had in the summer, but instead seemed to dance lightly on the red and gold leaves as they moved faintly in the breeze. It was the kind of autumn day that makes you happy to be alive.

(2) Students trying to write a composition often have trouble getting started. They chew on their pencils or stare at their computer screens, but no words come to mind. Experienced writers, too, may start on a piece of writing but then "get stuck" and be unable to think of anything to write next. A friend recently told me that he had finished his Ph.D. dissertation a year late because, for a while, his thoughts stopped coming when he faced a computer. Even professional writers can sometimes suffer from "writer's block": the condition of being unable to start or go on writing. Sometimes these problems are caused by tiredness or a lack of deep interest in the subject, but in other cases a writer may feel awake and interested and still be stuck for words. The best solution is to stay calm. Take a little break from writing—go for a walk, or listen to some music—and remember that writer's block is a common problem—it does not mean that you will never write again! No writer finds writing easy all the time.

In the first example, the topic sentence is like a kind of title or headline. In the second one, it sums up the content of the paragraph. It would also be possible to begin the second paragraph with the topic sentence "No writer finds writing easy all the time" and end it with the words "you will never write again!"

II. The Topic Sentence

Actually, topic sentences are not absolutely necessary. As you read more and more English during your college years, you will often find paragraphs which do not have definite topic sentences. *If* the writer had one clear central idea in mind for the paragraph, and *if* that idea is clear to readers, then probably the lack of a topic sentence does not matter. However, topic sentences are very helpful for both readers and writers, and until you become very good at writing English you should always try to include a topic sentence in each paragraph.

To understand why topic sentences are so helpful, read the following paragraph and try to tell what the writer's assertion is.

(3) College classes meet only once a week, and the content is often far more difficult than anything the students have done before. Although there may be weekly homework, there are few quizzes or regular tests, so that almost everything depends on the final test. Most professors place less emphasis on the memorization of facts than on how the student analyzes those facts. Just doing the homework the teacher assigns and remembering what the teacher says are no longer enough—students need to make an effort on their own to build their knowledge or develop their skills. This issue of initiative—that students must now take a major part of the responsibility for their own learning—is perhaps the biggest difference of all.

What is the writer's central idea? Probably you could tell that the topic of this paragraph is studying in college. But what does the writer want to say about college classes? What assertion is being made? If you are a very good reader and a very good guesser, you may have seen that the writer wanted to tell about the differences between studying in high school and studying in college. But don't you think that the following paragraph is much easier to understand?

(4)   Studying in college is quite different from studying in high school. College classes meet only once a week, and the content is often far more difficult than anything the students have done before. Although there may be weekly homework, there are few quizzes or regular tests, so that grades depend almost entirely on the final test. Most professors place less emphasis on the memorization of facts than on how the student analyzes those facts. Just doing the homework the teacher assigns and remembering what the teacher says are no longer enough—students need to make an effort on their own to build their knowledge or develop their skills. This issue of initiative—that students must now take a major part of the responsibility for their own learning—is perhaps the biggest difference of all.

Now readers can see immediately that the important point is the *difference* between studying in high school and studying in college. The connection between the rest of the sentences becomes clear, too: all of them help to show why the writer thinks studying in college is so different. A clear topic sentence helps the reader understand more easily. This is very important, because in English writing, the writer is responsible for making ideas clear to the reader. In English, you must not rely on *ishindenshin*!

II. The Topic Sentence

> Some writers of textbooks say—
>
> —That in English, the writer has the responsibility for making the meaning clear so that the reader can understand easily.
> —That in Japanese, writers tend to be vague, to be poetic, and give only hints. The reader has the responsibility of making connections in order to discover the main points.
>
> What do you think? Do you agree?

A topic sentence helps not only readers but also writers. One of the first things writers must do is to decide what to include in a paragraph and what to leave out. This is much easier to do if they write a topic sentence which limits their subject to *one* topic and *one* assertion about that topic. If writers do this, they will have set up boundary lines which help them decide what to write in the rest of the paragraph, and which help the readers as well.

Since topic sentences are so useful, let's think a little more carefully about how to write a good topic sentence. Do you think the sentence "Mito is my hometown" would be a good topic sentence? The answer is no, because this sentence would not help the writer decide what to write in the rest of the paragraph. The writer could write about what there is to like (or hate) about Mito, about the products Mito is famous for, or about the distance between Mito and Tokyo. In other words, this sentence contains no controlling central idea. It would not help the writer. Of course, it would not help the reader, either. It would be no good at all as a topic sentence.

But let's suppose a student called Yuri really does want to write about the topic of Mito, which is her hometown. Suppose Yuri adds an assertion which needs some proof or some explanation. She could change the topic sentence to, say, "Mito is famous for the *ume* (plum) trees in Kairakuen Park." This sentence would be a much better guide, for it would help Yuri remember that she should give only facts which will tell readers about the fame of those *ume* trees. Yuri may write about the great number of people who visit Kairakuen each year to see the blossoms. She may tell about the many scenes of the *ume* blossoms in Kairakuen shown on national television each year. She may mention the number of trees, or the great variety of trees. In any case, it is clear that only information which is related to the fame of the *ume* trees in Kairakuen should be included.

This topic sentence would also help Yuri's readers, because it would tell them what to expect; knowing what to expect, they would be able to read more easily and understand more quickly.

EXERCISE 1. Read the pairs of sentences below and in each case decide which one would be a better topic sentence.

    a. i. Tokyo is the capital of Japan.
       ii. Tokyo is one of the economic capitals of the world.

    b. i. Machi Tawara is a *waka* poet.
       ii. Machi Tawara started a new style of *waka*.

    c. i. A great earthquake may occur anywhere, anytime in Japan.
       ii. There are several precautions that we can take against

earthquakes.

   d. i. Whenever I stayed at my grandmother's house, I learned a lot about the customs of rural Japan.
      ii. When I was in elementary school, I used to stay at my grandmother's house during the summer vacation.

   e. i. My uncle lives on Hachijojima Island.
      ii. My uncle is very glad that he lives on Hachijojima Island.

EXERCISE 2. Underline the topic sentence in each of the following paragraphs.

a.   My friend Aya was an ideal high school student. She always seemed to get good grades, whether in English, history, or math, without studying too much. Her kindness and sense of humor made everyone like her, and she was chosen for many leadership positions. She was also a good athlete, and seemed to pick up the skills needed for volleyball, tennis, and skiing much faster than the rest of us.

b.   There are many environmental problems in our world. We keep on generating too much trash every day. Extreme weather caused by climate change is threatening our food supply. Our forests are dying, and our rivers and oceans are becoming polluted. The air may soon be too dirty to breathe in some places. The earth's biodiversity is in danger, and the loss of plant and animal species poses a serious threat to the health of our ecosystems.

c. It used to be that Japanese liquor shops sold only four or five kinds of beer—all lagers. Then in the 1970s, companies began to experiment. They tried producing malt beers and dark ales. They began to sell bottled draft beer. Then came light beers, beers that were created to taste good in winter, and even a beer that was supposed to go well with one kind of cooking—*nabemono*, or one-pot cooking. The most recent trend is the production of craft beer, which is beer made by small, local breweries in traditional or non-mechanized ways. Japan now has a great many kinds of beer.

d. What is *okara*? This is the name of the crumbly, moist, off-white material that you see steaming in heaps outside your local tofu shop early in the morning. It is soy pulp fiber, a byproduct of making soy milk. Although it is not as high in protein as soybeans, it is still an excellent source of protein. *Okara* is widely eaten in Japan; in the West, where it is valued for its taste and fiber, it is added to cereals, baked in cookies, and even made into sausage.

e. We all know that there are many working mothers in today's Japanese society. They work to pay the bills, to support their families, and to develop their careers. But if given the choice, is this what women really *want* to do? During the mid-1970s the number of working mothers was relatively low as many Japanese women chose to quit their jobs once they got married. Becoming a housewife and a stay-at-home mother was an ideal life path for many women at that time. But things have changed. According to a recent survey, 86% of Japanese women want to continue working after having children, although the percentage of those who do so is lower due to the challenges many working mothers face. It is apparent that in Japanese society today, most women want to work and want to continue working even after starting a family.

f. Activities give students an opportunity to express themselves in group work and to act as leaders and members of teams. When they participate in discussions, they become less self-conscious and more confident of their own abilities and ideas. Moreover, students enjoy working on projects, such as decorating for dances or putting on political campaigns. They find a great deal of satisfaction in doing their jobs well, and all of this serves its purpose in preparing them for assuming responsibility in adult life. For these reasons, every student should participate in at least one extracurricular activity.

EXERCISE 3. Look again at paragraph (2) on p. 8. Would you prefer to put the topic sentence at the beginning or at the end? How would the feeling of the paragraph change if the topic sentence were at the beginning? Which position makes the paragraph easier to understand?

EXERCISE 4. The following sentences probably would not make very good topic sentences. Why? Rewrite them so that they include an effective assertion.

  a. The Beatles' songs are really wonderful.
  One suggestion: The Beatles brought great changes to the music industry.

b. Japanese students have to study history in high school.

c. My grandmother's cooking is the best in the world.

d. Many people are discussing ways to improve the Japanese economy.

e. Traveling abroad is interesting.

f. Deciding on a career is an important step in life.

EXERCISE 5. <*Suggested Writing*> Jot down as many ideas as you can about your hometown (or a city you know well). You can include famous spots, places you like which aren't famous at all, interesting things to do, problems the city faces—anything! After you have written down as many as you can think of, circle some which are closely related, write a topic sentence which covers those ideas, and then try to write a paragraph using that topic sentence.

III. The Rest of the Paragraph

Now you know that a good paragraph usually has a topic sentence, and that the topic sentence often comes at the beginning and announces the paragraph's assertion. What is in the rest of the paragraph?

In order to answer that question, let's look once more at the paragraph about the environment which appeared on p. 13.

(5) There are many environmental problems in our world. We keep on generating too much trash every day. Extreme weather caused by climate change is threatening our food supply. Our forests are dying, and our rivers and oceans are becoming polluted. The air may soon be too dirty to breathe in some places. The earth's biodiversity is in danger, and the loss of plant and animal species poses a serious threat to the health of our ecosystems.

Here, as the topic sentence, the writer has stated the opinion that there are many environmental problems. The rest of the sentences in the paragraph are used to **support** that opinion. Here is a list of the six ideas that support the writer's opinion about environmental problems:

1. We generate too much trash.
2. Climate change is causing extreme weather that threatens our food supply.
3. Our forests are dying.
4. Our rivers and oceans are becoming polluted.
5. The air (is dirty and) soon may be too dirty to breathe in some places.
6. The loss of biodiversity is threatening the health of our ecosystems.

The writer has arranged these six ideas into five **supporting sentences** which tend to validate the assertion that there are many environmental problems.

Now, let's think about the number of sentences in the paragraph and the number of supporting sentences. The paragraph above contains only a topic sentence and supporting sentences. We could show the relationship between the topic sentence and the supporting sentences like this:

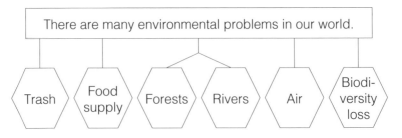

The example above is clear and effective; however, not all paragraphs have these good qualities. Read the paragraph below, find the topic sentence, and draw lines under the supporting sentences.

III. The Rest of the Paragraph

(6)	There are two common reasons for buying a bicycle. Some people buy a bicycle because it is practical to have one. Others buy a bicycle for sports and so on.

This paragraph is easy to read and analyze, isn't it? It is so simple that it probably seems completely uninteresting. Furthermore, the writer's ideas aren't very well explained because they lack detail. What makes it "practical to have" a bicycle? This paragraph suffers from **inadequate development**. Let's try again. Read the following paragraph, find the topic sentence, and draw lines under the sentences which support the topic sentence. (Each sentence has been numbered for convenience.)

(7)	^{1}People buy bicycles for many different reasons, but there are two common ones. ^{2}Some people need a bicycle for practical, everyday purposes such as cycling to school or going to the shops. ^{3}Buyers like this normally buy a bicycle that is reliable, not too expensive, and equipped with a basket for carrying things. ^{4}Others want a bicycle for sports and recreation. ^{5}These kinds of cyclists are willing to purchase more expensive bicycles to get the features that they need, such as light materials for racing bicycles or wide tires and durable materials for mountain bikes.

It is probably clear to you that the first sentence is still the topic sentence. Now, which sentences did you underline as supporting sentences? If you chose the second and the fourth sentences, you are right. These two sentences, which explain the topic sentence, are similar to the second and third sentences in paragraph (6). Then what about the third and fifth sentences? Should they have been included? Or are they mistakes?

No, of course they are not mistakes. Look at the following outline:

1. _____.
    2. _____.
        3. _____.
    4. _____.
        5. _____.

Or, we could sketch it like this:

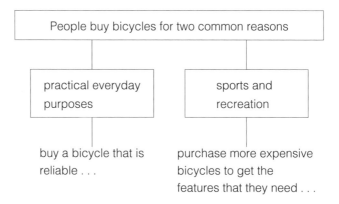

As you can see from the outline and the sketch, the third sentence supports the second one, and the fifth sentence supports the fourth one. So this paragraph has two main supporting sentences, and two other sentences which explain, or **develop**, the supporting sentences. Another way to describe this paragraph is to say that sentence 1 is the most general, sentences 3 and 5 are the most specific, and sentences 2 and 4 are in between.

Now, let's look at one final example. As you read it, see if you

III. The Rest of the Paragraph

can find the topic sentence and the two supporting ideas.

(8)   ¹Life has become harder and harder for small bookstores in the past twenty or thirty years. ²For one thing, it has become difficult to compete with online stores. ³Although some people still like to visit a physical store and inspect a book carefully before they buy it, many others prefer the convenience of buying a book online. ⁴Another problem is that small bookstores cannot offer an enormous variety of books. ⁵Therefore, if a book is rare, people normally try to find it online. ⁶But the competition with online stores is not the only problem for small bookstores. ⁷A second challenge is that e-books are becoming increasingly popular: instead of reading printed books, many people are reading e-books on their smartphones or tablet computers. ⁸They always carry devices like these with them anyway, and an e-book does not add any weight to their bags. ⁹Price is another consideration: an e-book is often a bit cheaper than a printed book, and thousands of classic novels and nonfiction classics can even be downloaded for free. ¹⁰For example, if you want to read one of Charles Dickens's famous novels, such as *A Christmas Carol*, you can download it from the *Project Gutenberg* website free of charge. ¹¹For reasons like these, it has become more and more difficult for small bookstores to survive.

It is probably clear to you that the topic sentence is the first one, and that the writer supports it with two main ideas:

1. It is difficult for small bookstores to compete with online stores.
2. People are reading more e-books and there is less

demand for the printed books that small bookstores sell.

Now, the next problem is the role of the other sentences. Can you put them in a simple outline like the one we provided for paragraph (7)? Try to do it yourself before you look at the suggested outline below!

1. _____.
  2. _____.
    3. _____.
    4. _____.
      5. _____.
  (6. _____.)
  7. _____.
    8. _____.
    9. _____.
      10. _____.
11. _____.

This is a very complicated paragraph, but you could probably see that sentences 3 and 4 support sentence 2. They both mention reasons why it is difficult for small bookstores to compete with online stores. And sentence 5 supports sentence 4 by explaining the problem that it mentions. Sentences 8 and 9 give two reasons why e-books are preferred to printed books, so they support sentence 7. Sentence 10 supports sentence 9 by giving an example of how you can download a classic novel for free.

How about sentence 11? If you think about it carefully, you will probably see that it says almost the same thing as the topic sentence. Since this paragraph is rather long, perhaps the writer decided to add 11 at the end as **a concluding sentence**, or summary, to remind readers of the main idea of the paragraph. It is as broad an idea as the topic sentence, so in the outline it is placed all the way to the left, at the same level of generality as sentence 1.

Finally, what about sentence 6? It has been half left out of the outline! This sentence tells us that the writer is going to change the subject from talking about the challenges posed by online bookstores to something else. It helps the reader prepare for that change. As you can see in the outline, this sentence is a kind of bridge between the first supporting idea and the second one. It is called **a transition**, or **a transitional sentence**.

A paragraph, then, is normally made up of a topic sentence followed by supporting sentences. In addition, there may be sentences which explain the supporting sentences, transitional sentences, and a concluding sentence. Together they develop one main idea—the idea which is expressed in the topic sentence.

EXERCISE 1. Here is one more rather complicated paragraph. See if you can make an outline or a sketch of it. How many main supporting ideas are there? Are there any transitional sentences? Is there a concluding sentence?

¹There is much evidence to support the view that Japan is the fastest-paced nation in the world. ²First, even a newcomer to the country soon notices that the people all seem to be in a rush. ³Pedestrians rush to avoid having to wait a minute or two at a stoplight. ⁴So do cars. ⁵Commuters run on crowded subway staircases, risking injury in order to save three minutes by catching the 8:21 instead of the 8:24. ⁶Noteworthy, too, is the reaction of the Japanese consumer to new products which can help them get information fast. ⁷A couple of decades ago, ordinary people seemed to accept products like answering machines and home fax machines almost immediately; they rushed out to buy them far sooner than the middle class in the United States. ⁸Nowadays, people cannot wait to get their hands on the latest smartphone models, and social media apps are extremely popular for keeping updated on what friends are doing. ⁹No matter whether they are going somewhere or trying to get information, the Japanese do not like to wait.

EXERCISE 2. <Suggested Writing> Go back to paragraph (5) on p. 17. As we have seen, it has one topic sentence and five supporting sentences, but none of the supporting sentences is further developed. See if you can add development for two or three of the supporting sentences. Then, since the paragraph will have become much longer, try to add a suitable concluding sentence so that it becomes a new—and greatly improved!—paragraph.

IV. Writing Your Own Paragraphs

Now you know something about the structure of English paragraphs. But knowing about their structure is not very helpful unless you can also write them yourself. This chapter contains a few hints to help you write good paragraphs of your own. First, there is a section which will show you some common methods of developing paragraphs, together with examples which you can use as models. After that, there is a section which will help you find ideas about topics you plan to write on.

A. Methods of Paragraph Development

Here is a list of methods which are commonly used to **develop** paragraphs, or to explain their assertions. Keep in mind, as you look at the list and read the examples which follow, that some of these methods are good for one kind of topic or one kind of writing, but not very good for others. Remember, too, that good writers often use more than one kind of method in a single paragraph.

1. Details or Facts
2. Division or Classification

3. Illustrations or Examples
4. Reasons
5. Comparison or Contrast
6. Definition
7. Problem-Solution
8. How-to-do-it
9. Chronological Order
10. Description

1. Details or Facts   (Can you give some facts about X?)

Giving facts, statistics, or other details can help readers understand the validity or the exact meaning of your assertion.

(9)   While Millennials are dieting just like generations before, concerns about the environment are influencing their dieting behavior. According to a January 2020 survey by YouGov, 20% of Millennials reported changing their diets in order to reduce their impact on the planet as compared to 13% of Gen Xers and 8% of Baby Boomers. Similarly, Millennials were also more likely to report they have tried a vegan diet, with 16% of Millennials going vegan at one point, compared to 7% of Gen Xers and 8% of Baby Boomers. These figures indicate that younger generations are growing increasingly concerned about sustainability. Some experts predict that for generations to come, choosing a diet that is good for the planet will be more than just a trend; it will be a defining lifestyle choice.

Source: https://today.yougov.com/consumer/articles/27476-millennials-diet-climate-change-environment-poll

IV. Writing Your Own Paragraphs

2. Division or Classification   (Can X be divided into types or groups?)

Analyzing things and then dividing them into groups is an important tool for understanding. It is something that both good business people and good scholars do. Do you remember this paragraph? It is a good example.

(10)   People buy bicycles for many different reasons, but there are two common ones. Some people need a bicycle for practical, everyday purposes such as cycling to school or going to the shops. Buyers like this normally buy a bicycle that is reliable, not too expensive, and equipped with a basket for carrying things. Others want a bicycle for sports and recreation. These kinds of cyclists are willing to purchase more expensive bicycles to get the features that they need, such as light materials for racing bicycles or wide tires and durable materials for mountain bikes.

3. Illustrations or Examples   (Can you give some examples to help explain X?)

A typical illustration tells a little story about someone, or about something that has happened.

Notice that the first paragraph below has just one long example, although writers often give several examples in order to be more convincing, as in paragraph (12) below.

(11)   While it used to be that living at home after graduating from college was a sign of failure, more and more young

Americans are choosing to live at home in order to achieve their personal and financial goals. Nina Cook, 23, moved back home to Boston after she became unhappy while working at her first job out of college. When she was living in New York City for her former job at an advertising company, she spent about $2,000 a month on rent and could barely save any money. Now, living at home with her mother and sister and working at a consulting company, Ms. Cook has been able to save around $1,500 a month. Although she feels secure enough to start looking for her own place again, she says she does not want to live too far from home.

(12)   Many of the old, fascinating sections of Tokyo are fast disappearing. This would appear to apply to many favorite tourist attractions as well. A visitor from India who had long been looking forward to visiting the small electrical appliance shops in Akihabara recently complained that the whole area seems to have been taken over by computer stores. "Besides, prices are no cheaper than in Shinjuku or Ikebukuro," he added. A middle-aged American scholar who comes to Japan once every six or seven years was equally disappointed by changes in the Kanda area. "I used to be able to find quality used books at low prices," she noted. "But now a lot of the most interesting small bookstores have gone out of business. I wonder if I'll ever bother to go again." The same phenomenon has struck the architecture of the city: one world traveler with an old guidebook was hoping to take pictures of some of Frank Lloyd Wright's creations. Alas! The Imperial Hotel was gone; he had to content himself with other architectural highlights. The lesson for the curious tourist would seem to be "See it quick

before it disappears!"

4. Reasons (Why?)

In both the examples below, the writers have given reasons to explain an action or a situation. There are also many cases in which writers use this method of development to explain why a certain opinion is right or wrong. Notice that in the first example here, there is no clear topic sentence. Does this make the main idea of the paragraph hard to understand?

(13)   My roommate has started playing music and dancing around the apartment first thing in the morning. She says that she is trying to have more "fun" in her life. She recently read the book *The Power of Fun* and learned that increasing fun is good for our mental and physical health. My roommate said that dancing is a good choice for her because she loves music and moving her body. She also told me that dancing in the morning will help her get in shape for the Dance Nuts performance at the school festival. Since I have a lot of assignments and can sometimes feel stressed, I think I might join in on her morning dances!

(14)   I joined a tennis club near my home in order to get some exercise, and promptly gained five kilograms. At first this was hard for me to understand, but I soon saw the connection. After one or two fun-filled sets, my friends and I would return to the clubhouse for a break. We would spend a pleasant hour there, chatting, sipping tea, and enjoying each other's home-baked cookies. Then we would return to the courts for more

tennis. On warm afternoons, we sometimes quenched our thirst with a glass or two of cold beer before going home. And on tennis days, since I was tired, hungry, and conscious of having gotten a lot of exercise, I would frequently overeat at suppertime. Tennis can be an excellent way to gain weight.

This last paragraph tells a little story about the writer, so it is similar to a paragraph developed by example. But "hard to understand" is a key phrase here—the writer wants to know *why*. If there had been a topic sentence like "People who play tennis with their friends as a hobby sometimes gain weight," then this might be taken as a paragraph developed by example; however, that is not the case here.

5. Comparison or Contrast   (How is X similar to, or different from Y?)

Comparison means pointing out the similarities between two things; contrast, on the other hand, means showing the differences. Often a writer uses only one or the other, but sometimes they are used together in the same paragraph.

(15)   Karaoke and pachinko are both very popular leisure activities in Japan and both require some skill, but there the similarity ends. The former is done for pleasure and brings no profit to the participants, but the latter is a form of gambling. Karaoke has grown popular in many other countries, but non-Japanese show little interest in pachinko. And finally, whereas karaoke is a social activity that people normally enjoy in groups, the pachinko player's passion is enjoyed alone. Indeed, the fact

that it is a solitary pursuit may be one of its attractions.

On examinations, teachers very often ask students to compare and contrast two people, two theories, or two situations. It is worth learning how to write good examples of this kind of paragraph.

6. Definition (What is X? What does X mean?)

Paragraphs developed by definition may be informative, like the first example, or they may be more subjective, like the second.

(16)   Club jazz, or acid jazz, is a mix of established styles and new sounds. It brings Latin rhythms and funky bass together with the melodies of traditional jazz instruments like the saxophone and the trumpet. This new, highly danceable sound was born in London in the 1980s. Live bands began to play alongside DJs in unplanned performances, thus creating the fresh, spontaneous feeling which is still a key part of club jazz today.
———based on *Cross Section*, No. 10

(17)   Jealousy is a poison. It is an acid cloud over the jealous person's life. It is a snake that gnaws at the heart, leaving it maimed and helpless. It is a rusty knife, ready to stab. It is an anonymous letter, a silent phone call in the dead of night. Jealousy is a poison.

7. Problem-Solution (Is there a problem about X? How can it be solved? Is the solution a good one?)

Much serious writing is about problems and how to solve them. As is usually the case, the following example begins with the problem. Can you find a topic sentence? Can you identify the sentences which discuss the solution and the sentences which show the writer's opinion (evaluation) of the solution?

(18)   "Period poverty" refers to the lack of access to menstrual products, including pads and tampons, due to financial constraints. This issue affects a significant number of individuals worldwide, particularly those who are low-income or marginalized. The consequences of period poverty are far-reaching, including negative impacts on physical health, well-being, education, employment prospects, and overall quality of life. Scotland has taken a progressive and proactive approach to solve this problem. In 2018, it became the first country to provide free menstrual products in schools and colleges, ensuring that young people have access to these essential items without any financial burden. This pioneering step has been instrumental in reducing stigma, normalizing conversations around menstruation, and empowering individuals. Moreover, Scotland has gone a step further by passing the Period Products Act in 2020. This legislation ensures that menstrual products are freely available in various public places, including community centers, libraries, and public toilets. More countries around the world should follow Scotland's lead in tackling period poverty and promoting menstrual equity.

8.   How-to-do-it   (How does a person do or make X?)

When you need to give this sort of explanation, keep things in the right order and be sure not to leave out any steps. It is particularly important to think about your readers. What will they not understand? The way the following instructions are written should be different for a Japanese and for a non-Japanese, don't you think?

(19)   You can make delicious miso soup in the following way. For four servings you need 40 grams of *niboshi* (small, dried fish for making stock), one cake of tofu, one piece of *aburaage* (fried tofu), one long onion, and 60 grams of miso. First, it is important to make good soup stock. Put the *niboshi* in five cups of water and let them simmer for about ten minutes. While the stock is simmering, prepare the ingredients. Pour hot water over the *aburaage* to remove the excess oil and then cut it into thin strips. Cut the onion crosswise into very thin slices and the tofu into one-centimeter cubes. Now, remove the pan from the heat. When the fish have settled to the bottom, pour the stock through a few layers of gauze to strain it. Then add the strips of *aburaage* and return the pan to the heat. Boil for about five minutes. Put the miso in a separate bowl, dissolve it with a ladleful of hot stock, and return the mixture to the pan. Add the tofu and heat the soup, but this time do not let it boil. Remove from the heat, ladle into bowls, and serve with the onion added.

9. Chronological Order   (How did X come about?)

This kind of writing is common in fiction, when the author tells what happened in a story. It also appears in newspaper accounts of events and in other kinds of nonfiction, such as biographies or encyclopedias. Topic sentences are rare in paragraphs developed chronologically. Instead, there are usually a great many words and phrases about time. How many can you find in this example?

(20)   Many years ago, there was a young American named Ranald MacDonald who wanted to see Japan. In 1847, when the Land of the Rising Sun was still closed to the outside world, he got a job on a whaling ship which was going to sail to Asia. One day, when his ship was passing northwestern Hokkaido, he got in a small boat and rowed away alone. He reached Yagishiri and Rishiri Islands safely, but was soon found and arrested by the Japanese. His captors sent him to Nagasaki, where he was kept locked up in a small room in a temple. While he was imprisoned, he passed the time by making a simple dictionary of English and Japanese words, and by teaching English to a few young Japanese who came to his room for lessons. He was finally sent home in 1849.

10. Description   (What is X like?)

This kind of writing is also common in fiction, where writers may use it to tell readers about a character's appearance or personality. Writers of both fiction and nonfiction need it to describe places and objects. In the example below—a novelist's description of an unusual character—there is no topic sentence, but some descriptive paragraphs do have one. (Look back at paragraph (1) on p. 8, for an example of a descriptive paragraph with a topic sentence.)

(21)   Doctor Parcival was a large man with a drooping mouth covered by a yellow mustache. He always wore a dirty white waistcoat out of the pockets of which protruded a number of the kind of black cigars known as stogies. His teeth were black and irregular and there was something strange about his eyes.

The lid of the left eye twitched; it fell down and snapped up; it was exactly as though the lid of the eye were a window shade and someone stood inside the doctor's head playing with the cord.   ——from Sherwood Anderson, *Winesburg, Ohio*

If someone asked you to write a topic sentence for paragraph (21), what would you write?

EXERCISE. Read the following paragraphs. If there is a topic sentence, underline it. Then try to decide which method of development it follows. (Remember that paragraphs are not simple things. A single paragraph may be a combination of several methods of development.)

a.   "Virtual fashion" is clothing and other fashion articles which only exist on computers and not in real life. Designers use special computer programs to make digital models of clothes and accessories. They can change and move these digital designs to create cool outfits and fashion shows. You can see virtual fashion on websites, social media, and even in virtual reality. You can try on virtual clothes using special apps or dress up characters in video games. It is good because designers can make unique and crazy things that would not work in real life. It is also better for the environment because it does not use up resources like making real clothes does. It is a new and exciting way to do fashion that mixes the real world and the computer world together.

b.   Playing a vinyl record is a delightful and nostalgic experience. To begin, place the record on the record player's turntable, ensuring it is free from dust or debris. Turn the power on and gently lift the arm and position it over the outer edge of the record. Lower the needle onto the spinning record's surface with care, allowing it to rest comfortably in the grooves. The music should start playing after the needle makes contact. When you are finished, lift the arm from the record, power off the turntable, and store the record safely in its sleeve. Enjoy the timeless charm of vinyl!

c. Professionals who have played the game in both countries say that American baseball and Japanese baseball are quite different. One of the first differences that non-Japanese players notice in Japan is the constant noise from the crowd. During a game in the United States, there are many quiet moments, but in Japan the cheering never seems to stop. On the field there are differences, too. Japanese players bunt more often. American pitchers throw more fast balls. The strike zone is different. American players in Japan almost all comment that in the U.S., pros save their energy for the game itself, while in Japan, players wear themselves out in practice before the game. A final difference is that Japanese players rarely change teams. Unlike players in the U.S., who are traded freely, Japanese players tend to remain loyal to the teams and fans that nurtured them over their careers.

d. Punctuation marks are like traffic signs which the writer provides for readers. When there is no punctuation, the reader should move ahead at a steady speed. Commas, semicolons, and periods tell the reader when to slow down and when to stop. Other punctuation marks, such as dashes, give hints about approaching turns and changes of direction. Good punctuation guides the reader smoothly along the written text. On the other hand, misplacement or omission of helpful punctuation marks can cause the reader to have to back up and start reading all over again, or, in the worst case, to get completely lost.

e. An old saying tells us that punctuality is the politeness of princes. We could just as well say that good punctuation is the politeness of writers. A well-placed comma tells the reader to breathe or pause for an instant. Semicolons, periods, and other end punctuation marks warn the reader to prepare for a new grammatical structure. Carefully used dashes and parentheses let the reader know that something is being inserted into the main grammatical structure of the sentence. Good punctuation helps the reader read smoothly, quickly, and accurately. It is an important resource that enables the writer to show good manners toward readers.

f. Japan is divided into four kinds of geopolitical areas, each of which may be considered a kind of prefecture. The one which comes to mind first is the *ken*. There are 43 *ken*, ranging from Okinawa in the south to Aomori in the northeast. Next, there are the *fu*. There are two of these prefectural areas—Kyoto and Osaka. Then there is one prefecture, Hokkaido, called a *dou*, probably because of its special administrative history in the days when it was considered a frontier area. Finally, there is a *to*, a label given only to the area including the modern capital, Tokyo, and its environs. Together, these 47 *todoufuken* make up the total land area of Japan.

g. Streaming music has mostly replaced the use of CDs as a way of enjoying music. While CDs offer tangible ownership and the ability to play music without requiring an internet connection, streaming allows users to access an extensive library of songs online, giving them instant and convenient access to a vast range of music. Streaming services offer personalized recommendations, curated playlists, and the ability to discover new artists easily. Unlike CDs, streaming does not require storage space or physical ownership, and it enables users to enjoy music on various devices with an internet connection. Overall, while CDs provide a tangible and high-quality music experience, streaming offers greater accessibility, convenience, and an extensive selection of music.

h.　　Almost all signs of its communist years have disappeared from Hungary. In the capital city of Budapest, the names of streets have been changed back to the names they had before World War II. In schools, everyone is learning English instead of Russian, which was a required subject until 1990. Entertainment has also gone Western. The last Russian TV station stopped broadcasting in February of 1994, and the most popular shows are now American programs like *Dallas** and *Columbo*.** The styles young Hungarians wear come from European fashion magazines and the American music channel MTV. There is little to remind people now of Hungary's forty odd years of communism.

――based on *Cross Section*, No. 10

*Dallas = a popular TV drama　　**Columbo =「刑事コロンボ」

i.　　What is a story? Erskine Caldwell defines it best as "an imaginary tale with a meaning, interesting enough to hold the reader's attention, profound enough to express human nature." It does not matter where the reader's attention has been directed, so long as it is stimulated and held. Our only concern as readers is, to paraphrase Chekhov, Did it keep you awake? Did it shock? Did it amuse? Did it send you away feeling you have had an experience more absorbing than any in your own life?

——Hallie Burnett, *On Writing the Short Story*

j.   Lawsuits, so common in the United States, do not have a very good reputation for effectiveness in Asian countries. Here is the story of one suit which occurred in Japan. A man named X wrote a book which criticized a famous Japanese company. Since his criticisms were largely false, were written in a sarcastic way, and harmed the company's sales and reputation, the company sued him. Ten years later the company won. But the amount of money they got was almost nothing, while the cost of the trial had been very great. Even worse, in the meantime, publicity about the lawsuit had made so many people curious that X's book sold very well, thus further damaging the company's reputation!

B. Finding Ideas

In the first part of this chapter, you read a number of paragraphs and analyzed the methods that their writers used. Hopefully you got some hints from these models about how to write your own paragraphs so that they will be well developed.

But in spite of what you have studied, you may still have trouble writing paragraphs. Knowing about structure (such as topic sentences) and methods of development (such as "how-to-do-it") is helpful, but it is not enough. Perhaps you are having trouble because you can't think of good ideas. To help you, we are now going to go back to what we've skipped over. In the first part of this chapter we looked at the final result. Now, let's return to the beginning and think about the processes that the writers of those paragraphs may have used to find their ideas.

Your teacher may tell you to write a paragraph on any topic you like. In that case, there are two important things to remember. One is to choose a subject that interests you, and the other is to choose a subject that you have some knowledge about. Or, your teacher may give you a specific topic to write about. But whether your topic is open or assigned, you will need things to write about in your paragraph. Here, let's use the topic of "The School Cafeteria" as an example of how to collect ideas.

Of course, by now you know that just having a topic is not enough. You need an assertion and supporting sentences. But before we start thinking about assertions for your paragraph on the school cafeteria, let's try an activity called **mind mapping** to find ideas. To help your brain start working, take out a pencil and see how far you can go with the set of circles below. Using your imagination, fill in the circles, add more lines and more circles as necessary, and just keep going. If there isn't enough space, begin again

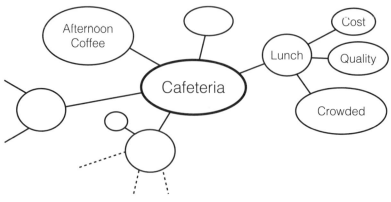

on another piece of paper.

When you have finished, look over the ideas you have jotted down. There are probably far too many ideas, and far too many kinds of ideas, for one paragraph. Try analyzing them to see what types of groups they fall into. Which ideas could go in the same paragraph? (For a fuller example of mind mapping, based on movies, see p. 87.)

EXERCISE 1. Draw a circle in the middle of a piece of paper and use mind mapping to gather ideas about one of the following topics:

   a. Money
   b. Child abuse
   c. Japan's relationship with the United States

EXERCISE 2. <Suggested Writing> Use the work you did in Exercise 1. Choose a few of the ideas which are very close together, write a topic sentence with a good assertion about the topic, and then write a paragraph.

*　　*　　*

Of course, mind mapping is not the only way to gather ideas. Another helpful method is to **ask yourself some general questions** about your topic and see which ones yield the most interesting (to you!) results.

Let's continue with the topic of the school cafeteria and use it to ask questions related to the methods of paragraph development that we studied above. Jot down answers to as many of the following questions as you can:

1. Do I know any facts or statistics about college cafeterias in general, or about our college cafeteria? Can I get some facts or statistics? What do my friends say about our college cafeteria?

2. Can college cafeterias be divided into types? What type is ours?

3. Do I know any interesting examples of things that have happened in our college cafeteria, especially things that would illustrate some point I want to make?

4. What are the reasons why our cafeteria is crowded/expensive, etc.? What are the reasons why this college has the kind of cafeteria that it has?

5. How is our college cafeteria similar to the ones at other colleges and universities? How is it different from the others?

6. What is a college cafeteria? What should a college cafeteria be?

7. Are there any problems about our cafeteria? If so, is there a solution? Is it a good solution?

8. Can I explain how to use our college cafeteria?

9. How did our college cafeteria come to be the way it is? Is

IV. Writing Your Own Paragraphs

there any story behind its history?

10. What is our cafeteria like? What is the best way to describe it to people who have never seen it?

Next, let's look at how one student named Emi answered a few of these questions. Here are her notes:

1. I could make a list of the food on the menu in our cafeteria, together with a list of prices. Maybe I could ask the manager of the cafeteria about the number of students who eat there, or get some other kind of data. I could distribute a questionnaire to students and get some facts about their use of our cafeteria and their opinion of it.

2. Some of them may be operated directly by the college, and others may be run by outside businesses for profit, but I don't know much about this. Not interesting.

3. I don't think I've heard any interesting or useful stories.

4. It's crowded because there aren't enough tables and chairs. The lunch period is too short. Another reason might be that some students save seats for their friends, and those seats can't be used by others. And some students stay in the cafeteria to study, so we can't use their chairs to eat. Why is it so expensive? I don't know.

5. I could compare or contrast our cafeteria to the cafeteria at my sister's university (ABC University), or perhaps to restaurants in town. But my sister's school is much bigger than ours, and at restaurants in town of course the situa-

tion is completely different.

6. A place to eat lunch. A place to have coffee and cake in the afternoon? A lot of students use our cafeteria as a place to study.

7. It's crowded and expensive. As for being crowded, I wonder if we could make rules about not saving seats or not studying in the cafeteria between noon and 1:00? Would rules like these work?

8. I know how to use the cafeteria. I know how to buy coupons from the machine and line up for what I want. I know where to get chopsticks and tea.

9. ?

10. I could write a very interesting description of our cafeteria! At 10:05 it's almost empty, and at 12:05 it's like a battleground!

Emi now has a lot of possible ideas for writing about the cafeteria. Actually, she has far too many ideas for one paragraph! Now she needs to decide on an assertion, and then she will need to decide what she wants to tell her readers about that assertion. What are some possible assertions?

(a) Our college cafeteria is not very popular.

(b) It will be easier for you to eat at our college cafeteria if you remember the following information. (Hours, cost, and hints about what kind of food is good.)

(c) ABC University has a far better cafeteria than ours.

(d) Our college cafeteria turns into a battlefield at 12:05 every weekday.

(e) Our college cafeteria is overcrowded. (Is there anything we can do about it?)

Now, what are some possible paragraphs that Emi might write using these ideas? Let's see what she did with the first one.

(22)   Our college cafeteria is not very popular. First, it is overcrowded. Every day, about 2,000 students eat lunch on campus, but the cafeteria has seats for only about 800 people. Also, because so many people try to eat there, it takes a long time to buy a coupon, go through the line, get one's food, and pick up tea. Another problem is lack of variety. There are only two kinds of set lunches, and they are almost the same every day. There are some other kinds of food besides set lunches, but they are usually all sold out by 12:15. The students' final complaint is that the food is rather expensive considering the quality. How can the cafeteria ask 700 yen for a set lunch that is mostly starch? And surely no restaurant in town would charge 500 yen for a bowl of overcooked noodles with almost no other ingredients.

Let's suppose she used the idea in (e). Could she explain the problem and consider a solution? In the paragraph below, she decided not to write about rules, but about the possibility of eating in classrooms.

(23)   Yamanote College, like most colleges whose campuses are at some distance from a shopping area, has a cafeteria where many of the students eat lunch. During the one-hour lunch break each day, about 2,000 students head for the cafeteria looking for a place to eat. Unfortunately, the cafeteria has only about 800 seats, and it is always seriously overcrowded during the noon hour, especially on rainy days when the students cannot eat outdoors. One solution which has been suggested is to allow the students to eat in classrooms near the cafeteria. Students could carry trays of food there easily, and there would be plenty of seats. However, the value of this solution would depend upon the behavior of the students themselves. Many teachers and other college workers fear that the students would not take trays, dishes, and empty drink cans back to the cafeteria—dirty classrooms would not be a solution.

If you are an analytical person, you have surely noticed that Emi's first paragraph is developed by giving reasons, and her second one is developed by using a problem-solution approach. However, Emi was probably not thinking about methods of development at all when she wrote these paragraphs. She was thinking about what she wanted to say. Her ideas led naturally to those methods of development. You, too, will probably find that your writing is much more successful if you write while concentrating on your ideas. Then, when you reread what you have written, think about the method(s) of development and see if you can make improvements.

On the following page, you will find a list of questions like the ones Emi tried to find answers to. These questions are a little different from the ones she used, and of course not all the questions will be useful for every topic. But this kind of list can be very help-

IV. Writing Your Own Paragraphs

ful. To use it, just replace "X" with your own topic. (As you can see, there is a close relationship between these questions and the methods of development you read about in the first half of this chapter.)

QUESTIONS TO ACTIVATE WRITERS' BRAINS

1. Do you know some facts or statistics about X? Can you get some facts or statistics by interviewing people, by looking at reference books, or by doing an online search? What do people, or the media, say about X?

2. Can X be divided into parts, types, or groups?

3. Can you give some good examples of X?

4. What are the reasons why X is good/bad/expensive, etc.? Why did a person do X? Why does a person believe X? What caused X to happen?

5. How is X similar to Y, or different from Y?

6. What is X? What is the opposite of X? What does X mean?

7. What is the problem about X? Is there a solution? Is the solution a good one? What would be the result of trying that solution?

8. How does a person do or make or use X?

9. How did X come about?

10. What kind of thing is X? What kind of person is X?

IV. Writing Your Own Paragraphs

EXERCISE 1. For further practice with a greater variety of paragraphs, look again at the examples which appeared in Chapters I-III. What kind of questions are they attempting to answer?

EXERCISE 2. Here are a few possible topics. Choose one, and then use the list of questions on p. 48 to try to find ideas. Make a list of three possible assertions about the topic you selected.

   a. Learning a foreign language
   b. A good restaurant for a class party
   c. Getting a seat on a train during rush hour
   d. Your class schedule

EXERCISE 3. <Suggested Writing> Using one of the ideas in Exercise 2, write a paragraph of your own. Include a topic sentence and supporting sentences. If you think it would be helpful, use either mind mapping or the list of questions on p. 48 to find ideas.

V. The Characteristics of a Good Paragraph

Now that you have learned what the parts of a paragraph are and have started to practice writing paragraphs yourself, it is time to think about some problems which are more advanced.

A. Unity and Consistency

One important quality that a good paragraph must have is **unity**. You have already learned that each paragraph must have a central, controlling idea. If all the sentences in the paragraph work together to express that one basic idea, then the paragraph has unity. If there are any sentences which do not help to develop the central idea, then the paragraph loses its unity.

In order to give a paragraph unity, you must keep to your topic and your assertion about that topic. It's probably obvious that if you begin to write a paragraph about earthquakes you should not suddenly begin to talk about shoe sizes unless the second idea helps to explain the first. You have to stick to one topic. But don't forget that you also have to stick to one assertion. To test your understanding of this point, read the following paragraph. Does it have unity?

V. The Characteristics of a Good Paragraph

(24)   English-English dictionaries for foreign students have many useful features. In addition to giving the meaning of common words together with their pronunciations, such dictionaries usually include many example sentences. They also have grammatical information and notes about usage so that students can learn to use the words correctly. I wonder which online dictionary I should use to improve my English. Finally, they also have a lot of information about a word's register—that is, whether a word is slang, formal, old-fashioned, or poetic.

Is everything in this paragraph about the same topic, dictionaries? Yes. Now, find the topic sentence. What assertion does it make? Does everything in this paragraph support that assertion? No. You were able to find the sentence that spoils the unity of the paragraph, weren't you?

Consistency deals with a similar problem. Paragraphs which are consistent have nothing contradictory in them. Read the next paragraph, which is very similar to one you have seen before. Do you think it is consistent?

(25)   My friend Junko was an ideal high school student. She always seemed to get good grades, whether in English, history, or math, without studying too much. Her kindness and sense of humor made everyone like her, and she was chosen for many leadership positions. She was also a good athlete, and seemed to pick up the skills needed for volleyball, tennis, and skiing much faster than the rest of us. Unfortunately, she was not good at music.

Did you notice that, while every other sentence in the paragraph says something good about Junko, the last sentence says something which is not? The last sentence spoils the consistency of this paragraph.

Does this mean that we can never mention a point which weakens our assertion? Not necessarily. Look at this rewritten version of the description of Junko's talents:

(26)　My friend Junko was an ideal high school student. She always seemed to get good grades, whether in English, history, or math, without studying too much. Her kindness and sense of humor made everyone like her, and she was chosen for many leadership positions. She was also a good athlete, and seemed to pick up the skills needed for volleyball, tennis, and skiing much faster than the rest of us. Although she was not good at music, she was so good at other things that even this weakness seemed rather charming.

Do you see how the writer has very skillfully used **a subordinate clause** to make the information that Junko was not good at music seem unimportant? Written in this way, information which appears contradictory can be prevented from harming consistency.

You must also be consistent about your point of view. The following kind of inconsistency is very common in beginners' English writing:

(27)　Following the "one in, one out" rule can help you to keep your room tidy. The rule is quite simple: whenever you buy something new, you must discard something old, preferably by recycling it. However, it is important to make sure that the new and old things are similar. If you want to buy a new pullover, you need to find an old pullover to recycle. We shouldn't buy a new pullover and discard an old sock with a hole in it. We would be cheating if we did this.

Most of the paragraph consists of advice from the writer of the paragraph to "you," the reader. But suddenly, in the last two sentences, the writer stops writing to "you" and starts using "we" instead. It would have been better to use a consistent point of view and write to "you" throughout the paragraph.

There are many other ways in which you should be consistent as a writer. If you are describing the *outside* of a building, you should not mention anything *inside* the building. If you begin to tell a story in the past tense, you should not change to the present tense. (In Japanese fiction, this is very common and of course it is not wrong. Japanese writing follows different conventions.) If you are writing something in formal English, you should not use slang or casual words.

B. Order

The concept of **order** is an easy one to understand. When telling a story, you keep things in good order by beginning with what happened first, then telling what happened next, and so on. But although the idea of **chronological order** is easy to understand, telling a story in good order is not always easy. Have you ever tried to explain the plot of an interesting movie to a friend? Maybe you forgot to give a few important pieces of information, added them later, and made your friend feel completely confused! Most people have had this kind of experience. It shows that telling things in the right order is not so easy—but very important.

Order is also very important when you explain how to do something. The following paragraph might not be very helpful, because it is not in chronological order. You will probably have to read it two or three times to figure out what you are supposed to do.

(28)   If you grow tomatoes in your garden, you should try making tomato sauce and preserving it in glass jars. First, make the tomato sauce. It is easy to find recipes for this on the Internet. Before canning the sauce in glass jars, you need to boil the jars to sterilize them. You can do this while you make the tomato sauce. Make sure to peel the tomatoes carefully before you boil them into a sauce! Then you pour the sauce into the jars until they are almost full, put the jars in a big pan of water, and boil them for an hour. Of course, you should fasten the lids carefully first. Leave the jars in the water to cool down until the following morning. If you do not grow tomatoes, buy some! Get tomatoes with low water content and few seeds, like San Marzano tomatoes.

Order is also important when a writer is describing a scene. It is very hard for readers to imagine a place which they cannot see and which is being explained to them in words only, without a picture. One way in which writers can help readers is by putting descriptions in **spatial order**. For example, a writer can describe things which are far in the distance first, and then describe things which are not so far away, and finally describe things which are very close. Or a writer could move from right to left. Or from top to bottom. In any case, it is important to help the reader by making the relative position of the things described clear. Read this example, taken from a novel:

(29)　　The little station, however, had not changed at all. Its shabby deserted little platform stood open to the sun; a black porter was cleaning the brown woodwork of the waiting room with a mop on a long handle. It was very quiet. She handed in her ticket, made her way out up the ramp to the street. The street was altered out of recognition. A new main road led to the new estate in one direction, back into old Romley in the other; it was designed for motorists and heavy lorries rather than pedestrians, but not impassable.
　　　　　　　　　　——Margaret Drabble, *The Middle Ground*

Here, the station at Romley is described in natural order, just as the woman (Kate) sees it when she gets off the train, moves along the platform to the exit, and then goes out to the street.

There are other important kinds of order. If you were writing a paragraph about three artists, would you begin with the most famous one, or end with the most famous one? If you were writing an editorial in favor of/against importing more rice from outside Japan, do you think it would be more effective to put the strongest reason first, or last?

C. Coherence

Coherence refers to the quality of being connected. If we say that a paragraph is coherent, we mean that "its parts fit together well so that it is clear and easy to understand" (*COBUILD English Dictionary*, 1987 ed.).

There are two kinds of coherence. The first, which is absolutely vital in a paragraph, is coherence of ideas. The idea in one sentence should lead logically to the idea in the next. The second kind of coherence might be called mechanical. When we use a series of expressions like *first*, *next*, and *finally*, we are using these words to make it easier for readers to understand how the ideas are connected. Of course, if the first kind of coherence is missing, it is useless to add the second! If there is no logical connection between the ideas in a paragraph, adding *first*, *second*, and *finally* won't help readers at all.

First of all, let's take a look at a paragraph which certainly does have logical coherence. That is, the ideas are smoothly connected.

(30)   Listening is a complex skill which takes time to acquire in a foreign language. You have to catch the speech sounds made by the speaker. You have to make sense of what you think you have heard. You may not be sure of some part of it. You have to guess. You have to keep asking yourself if what you think you have heard matches the context. All these steps proceed almost simultaneously, making listening a difficult process.

If we think hard about what the writer intended to say, this paragraph seems to be perfectly coherent as far as its *ideas* are concerned. But readers have to work to find the connection between the writer's ideas. This writer did not try very hard to help readers of the passage. Suppose, on the other hand, that the writer had written it in the following way, adding the underlined words and phrases:

(31)   Listening is a complex skill which takes time to acquire in

V. The Characteristics of a Good Paragraph

a foreign language. <u>First of all,</u> you have to catch the speech sounds made by the speaker. <u>Next,</u> you have to make sense of what you think you have heard, <u>though</u> you may not be sure of some part of it. <u>In that case,</u> you have to guess. <u>At the same time,</u> you have to keep asking yourself if what you think you have heard matches the context. <u>To make matters worse,</u> all these steps proceed almost simultaneously, making listening a difficult process.

The ideas have not changed, but now the underlined parts have been added as guideposts for the reader. With this mechanical coherence added to the logical coherence already present in paragraph (30), wasn't it easier to understand the relationship between one sentence and the next?

Since coherence is so important, let's consider four easy ways to add mechanical coherence to a paragraph. Of course, we assume that it already has logical coherence.

1. Use transitional adverbs, transitional adverbial phrases, and conjuctions, such as *meanwhile, however, therefore, first, second, third, after that, for example, although, because,* etc. Such words and phrases help readers see clearly how each sentence (or clause) is connected to the idea in the sentence(s) (or clause) before it.

2. Use pronouns, when the antecedent is clear, to remind readers of the subject of the previous sentence, or of other important words in it. When you do this, you link words in a new sentence to ideas in an old sentence. This helps to tie the whole paragraph together. It also helps the reader keep earlier ideas in mind.

3. Repeat key words, or words which are closely related to the key words, or words which are often paired, or words which are opposites. This has the same effect as using pronouns. Here are some examples:

> Salt is a chemical compound occurring naturally in many countries of the world as well as in seawater. Pepper, on the other hand, is a spice obtained from the berries of certain plants. (words often paired)
>
> Avoid threatening words and gestures. Such words and gestures . . . (key words)
>
> The curtain rose. At the back of the stage . . .
> (closely related words)
>
> Mechanically, there are four easy ways to achieve coherence. These mechanical techniques will help writers to link . . .
> (closely related words)

4. Repeat the same sentence patterns. This technique, though very effective, must not be used too often. Here is an example. What patterns are repeated in it?

(32)   Shunichi Saito is a very talented student. In June, he and his partner won first place in the national collegiate badminton championships. In September, he was chosen to appear in an amateur singing contest on television. And in December, he was notified that he had been awarded a scholarship to study philosophy in England.

In this paragraph, the pattern [in + (month)] is repeated three

V. The Characteristics of a Good Paragraph

times before the subject. The pronoun "he" appears three times as the subject (although the first time it appears with "his partner"). And finally, in the last two sentences, both these patterns are combined with passive verbs to form a sentence rhythm which remains in our minds:

<u>In September,</u> <u>he</u> <u>was chosen</u>
<u>in December,</u> <u>he</u> <u>was notified</u>

But remember that real coherence cannot be achieved just by using these mechanical techniques. If you think that only mechanical links are enough, look at the following paragraph. Is each sentence linked mechanically to the one before it?

(33) Yayoi Kusama is world famous for the way she uses polka dots in her works of art. <u>Works of art</u> are bought by rich art collectors for their private collections or displayed in museums. Some <u>museums</u>, such as the British Museum, are a major attraction for tourists. Lots of <u>tourists</u> visit Japan to enjoy skiing in winter. <u>This is a season</u> associated with Christmas in many countries around the world.

The answer is yes—each sentence is connected by the underlined words to the sentence before it. But it should be clear to you that this is a terrible paragraph. Why? It is because this is only a collection of sentences which are not controlled by a single topic or assertion.

Likewise, if your ideas do not flow naturally one after another, then your paragraph will not be coherent no matter how many transitional words and phrases you use. But if your paragraph already has coherent ideas put down in good order, it can be made structurally stronger and easier to read if you use the above techniques carefully.

EXERCISE 1. Read the following paragraph. Are there any sentences which weaken its consistency? If so, can you solve the problem by the use of a subordinate clause? (Some rewriting will also be necessary.)

> The ESS, to which I belong, is a very good club. The older students all do their best to help us first-year students, and they teach us many things. The other day, when I was very worried because I couldn't think of a topic for the next speech contest, the club president, Ayaka Sakamoto, gave me several good ideas. Only one student, a junior, sometimes criticizes us beginners and says that we are too stupid to take part in speech contests and debates. I have made friends with almost all the members of the club, and I enjoy going to the clubhouse just to meet and talk with them.

EXERCISE 2. Rewrite this paragraph so that it has unity and consistency.

> It is wonderful to have a car. I can go right to the place where I want to go. But sometimes I have trouble finding a place to park. It is also nice to be able to leave whenever I'm ready instead of having to get to the station by a certain time. Another good thing

about traveling by car is that I can take a lot of luggage. Driving on the expressways gives me a great sense of freedom. I especially like driving on the Chuo Expressway or the Tohoku Expressway because the scenery is so beautiful. What I do not like is the high cost of using the expressways. And gasoline is expensive, too.

EXERCISE 3. Look back at the paragraph about making tomato sauce and preserving it on p. 54. Rewrite it in good order so that readers will be able to follow the instructions more easily.

EXERCISE 4. Read these three paragraphs and follow the instructions that you find at the end.

a. Morihiro Hosokawa was an unusual prime minister. He was not a member of the Liberal Democratic Party. He showed a willingness to apologize frankly for some of Japan's actions during World War II. He had a likeable smile. He had a sense of fashion, and at the time of the 1993 APEC meeting in Seattle, many Japanese were pleased to see their leader looking just as stylish in his casual clothing as any of the other Asia-Pacific leaders attending.

b. Morihiro Hosokawa was an unusual prime minister. Politically, he was not a member of the Liberal Democratic Party. Perhaps for this reason, he showed a willingness to apologize frankly for some of Japan's actions during World War II. Personally, he had a likeable smile. He also had a sense of fashion, and at the time of the 1993 APEC meeting in Seattle, many Japanese were pleased to see their leader looking just as stylish in his casual clothing as any of the other Asia-Pacific leaders attending.

c.   Morihiro Hosokawa was an unusual prime minister. First, he was not a member of the Liberal Democratic Party, which had governed the country for over forty years. Second, the new prime minister surprised both his own nation and the world by his willingness to apologize frankly for some of Japan's actions during World War II. He also presented a new, more modern style as prime minister, as was evident at his press conferences, which he conducted standing and at which he made skillful use of teleprompters. Finally, the former Kumamoto governor had a more colorful personality than the Japanese were used to seeing in their leaders. This was evident in his likeable smile. It also showed up in his sense of fashion. At the time of the 1993 APEC meeting in Seattle, for example, he pleased many Japanese by looking just as stylish in his casual clothing as any of the other Asia-Pacific leaders attending. In all these ways, Hosokawa was quite different from most previous Japanese prime ministers.

1. Does paragraph a. have logical coherence? Does it have mechanical coherence?

2. Paragraphs b. and c. are rewrites of paragraph a. How do the three paragraphs differ? Which one shows the connections between ideas most clearly? Which one do you like best?

3. Look at paragraph c. again and make a list of all the words and phrases that are used to refer to Hosokawa.

4. Next, in paragraph c., underline all the words and phrases which seem to provide mechanical connections.

5. <*Suggested Writing*> Now, using the above paragraphs for reference, choose some well-known person whom you are interested in and write a paragraph highlighting this person's positive (or negative) characteristics.

After you have finished, use the "Paragraph Checklist" on the next page to see if there are any ways in which you can improve your paragraph even further.

Paragraph Checklist

✓   Did I indent at the beginning of the paragraph?
___ I didn't indent anywhere in the middle of the paragraph, did I?
___ Do I have a clear topic sentence? Does it make an assertion?
___ Do the other sentences in the paragraph support my assertion well?

*   *   *

___ Is there anything in my paragraph that harms its unity or consistency?
___ Does my paragraph have suitable transitional words or phrases to help readers understand the direction of my thought? (*first, therefore, in particular, for example*, etc.)
___ Have I used pronouns to strengthen coherence?
___ Have I presented my ideas in the most effective order?

*   *   *

___ Have I checked the spelling of words I'm not sure about?
___ Do all the verbs agree with their subjects?

*   *   *

___ Have I done everything I can to help the reader?
___ Would I enjoy reading this paragraph if someone else had written it?

VI. From the Paragraph to the Whole Essay

You have now spent quite a bit of time learning about paragraphs, reading paragraphs, and actually writing paragraphs. But the truth of the matter, as you probably know, is that most people who want to express something in writing do not write just one paragraph. A single paragraph is too short and too limited a unit to express complex aspects of a person's thinking about an issue. Next, therefore, it is time to find out how to put paragraphs together to create a longer piece of writing.

The two most important things to learn about essays, or multi-paragraph compositions, are how they are structured and how each paragraph is connected to the one before it.

A. The Structure of the Essay

Good full-length essays are in many ways similar to good paragraphs. Just as good paragraphs often contain a topic sentence, so do well-constructed essays begin with **an introductory paragraph** which normally contains **the thesis statement**, or the main idea of the essay. Like topic sentences, thesis statements should be specific: they should tell readers as clearly as possible what you intend to do in your composition. If your thesis statement, for example, is "Apartments in Utsukushiki Mansion are selling rapidly because of the convenient location, the reasonable cost, and the solid, resident-friendly construction," you have a good guide to follow in writing the rest of your composition.

In previous exercises in this book, you have been asked to write three or four sentences which supported, or developed, your topic sentence. Now, for the above thesis statement, you will probably write three or more **supporting paragraphs** which explain it in greater detail. You will probably write one paragraph to explain the convenience of the building's location. That paragraph may contain some ideas like these:

- (a) It is within walking distance of one JR station and two subway stations.
- (b) A bus stops right in front of the building.
- (c) It is near a shopping area.
- (d) Several schools are located nearby.

In the next paragraph you will probably focus on cost. Perhaps the individual condominiums are a little cheaper than others for sale in the same area. Perhaps the price range is just right for young couples with one or two children. And in the paragraph after that you will probably write about the building's earthquake-proof construction, the handy layout of the kitchens, and the pleasantly landscaped area in front of the building.

None of this should be difficult for you, however, because each of the supporting paragraphs mentioned above will be very similar to the ones you have already practiced writing. These supporting paragraphs should still have topic sentences, unity, continuity, and

VI. From the Paragraph to the Whole Essay

all the other qualities of a good paragraph which you have learned about earlier in this book.

Another similarity between independent paragraphs and longer compositions is the way they end. Although we have mentioned it only briefly, a paragraph often has a concluding sentence which restates the idea of the topic sentence in different words. A good essay, too, should end with **a concluding paragraph** which leaves readers with a sense of completion. It usually reminds readers of the main points, repeats the thesis statement in different words, and neatly ties the whole essay together.

Let's look at an example. Read the following passages about credit cards and then tell which sentences in paragraph (34) and which parts of essay (35) correspond to each other. (The sentences in (34) and the paragraphs in (35) have been numbered to make it easier for you to talk about them.)

(34)   [1]Every year a large number of people go bankrupt because they have used their credit cards unwisely. [2]One reason is the pressure of consumerism*, which many Japanese seemed to accept as their religion in good economic times. [3]A second reason is the proliferation of cards, which makes it easy for a person who needs money to borrow with one card to pay money owed on another. [4]A final factor is the effort of credit companies to encourage young people to get cards. [5]Eager to buy but inexperienced at handling money, many college students and young workers soon find themselves drowning in debt. [6]These are the main factors behind the increase in the number of credit card bankruptcies.

*consumerism = the belief that buying things and spending money are good

(35)   ¹Visitors to Japan in the 1970s were often amazed to find that the people here rarely used checks or credit cards, but instead paid for almost everything in cash. By the early 1980s, however, all that began to change as the Japanese discovered the convenience of plastic money. By 1983 there were 57 million credit cards in use, and by 1991 that number had jumped to 187 million. The number of cards has continued to grow— but so has the number of people who have used their cards unwisely and cannot pay their debts. Why has this happened? Consumerism, the proliferation of credit cards, and the increase in the number of young, inexperienced users are among the main reasons.

²Much of the blame for the current situation can be put on the new religion which Japan first adopted during good economic times—consumerism. Magazines, TV, friends, and even the government seemed to be encouraging people to buy. Shopping became a favorite leisure activity. New products were assumed to be better than old ones. Things which broke were to be replaced, not repaired. Buying was good, it seemed, and people bought a lot.

³Another problem is the number of cards being used. Even back in 1991, the Japanese had an average of 1.5 cards per person (including babies, children, and the very old); the number has risen so rapidly that it is not uncommon for one adult to have five or more different credit cards. As a result, Credit Card Company A may think that a customer's debt is only 500,000 yen, when in fact the customer owes that much on each of his or her cards. A further result of the proliferation of cards is that it is easy for a person to borrow with one credit card to pay money owed on another. Eventually such multiple

users may find that they are drowning in the total of their debt.

⁴A third factor which has made the situation worse is the large number of young credit card users. College students and first-time workers are good customers for the card companies because they are fashion-conscious, eager to have the good things of life, and diligent in shopping; knowing this, the companies have worked hard to encourage them to get cards. Unfortunately, many of them are also inexperienced at handling money or balancing a budget, and have tended to spend more every month than they can repay.

⁵There are many reasons for Japan's increasing bankruptcy rate among individuals, but the three mentioned above are the most serious. Unless consumerism is tamed, credit card companies are forced to give cards only to those able to pay, and the young are trained in the dangers of overspending, we may expect to hear more and more sad stories of people whose lives and reputations were ruined because of improper credit card use.

It was probably fairly easy to see the correspondence between certain sentences in (34) and certain paragraphs in (35). Of course, the correspondence is not perfect. For example, in (34), you probably found the topic sentence right where you expected to find it—at the beginning. But where did you find the thesis statement in (35)? It wasn't at the beginning, was it? And in essays, it usually isn't.

The credit card essay that you just read was written to follow a five-paragraph essay pattern that is very useful for both native speakers of English and learners of English as a second or foreign language. It is a very important pattern, because it shows clearly that single paragraphs and longer compositions are similar in many ways. But it is still very simple. The English writing that you will read in college is not likely to be so simple. Nor will most of your own essays be just five paragraphs.

Next, then, let's look at the ways in which longer pieces of writing *cannot* be compared to paragraphs. First, the introductory paragraph of a composition is more than just a statement of the main idea of the essay; that is, it is not just a "topic paragraph." In non-academic writing, it often begins with an eye-catcher which attracts the readers' attention and makes them want to read on.

EXERCISE. What is your opinion of the following openings? Would they make you feel interested in reading more? Are some of them boring?

    a. Aisha Khurram had to flee her home country just to get an education.
(At the beginning of an essay about educational rights for women in Afghanistan.)

    b. Do you believe that the earth is flat? Surprisingly, there are people who do.
(At the beginning of an essay about misinformation and the internet.)

    c. The most frequent visitors to Inokashira Park are crows.
(At the beginning of an essay saying that the government should do something to control crows.)

    d. Tokyo is a huge city with a population of more than four-

teen million people in 2023.
(At the beginning of an essay about moving the capital.)

After an opening which they hope is interesting, writers usually become more and more specific, and then end the introductory paragraph with their thesis statement.

The concluding paragraph, too, is more complicated than a concluding sentence in a paragraph. It should not contain new suggestions or reasons, but at the same time it should not be just a rewording of the thesis statement with a summary of the essay's main ideas added, either. It should also end strongly, perhaps with a quotation, a warning, or a call to action which will leave a lasting impression on the reader.

A final difference between single paragraphs and essays is that essays very often contain transitional paragraphs. (Paragraphs, of course, sometimes contain transitional sentences. Look back at p. 23.) The role of a transitional paragraph, as you may have guessed, is to help the writer (and the reader!) cross the gap between the idea of one group of paragraphs and that of the next. It is a kind of bridge. It shows that the writer is moving from one stage of an argument to the next.

B. Connections between Paragraphs

Do you remember, from reading pp. 55–60, that it is important to have connections (in mechanical structure and among ideas) within a paragraph? Similarly, the paragraphs in an essay should also be linked. It is obvious that the idea of one paragraph should be related in some way to the idea of the paragraph before it, and of course the use of words and phrases which make this relationship clear is very helpful to the reader. Let's look at some of the most common methods of using words and phrases to make the relationship of ideas clearer.

1. Numbering

One of the most common relationships between paragraphs is that they are parts of a list; the easiest way to show this relationship is to use the words *first, second,* and *third,* or *first, next,* and *finally.* Look ahead to the essay about the *tanshin-funin* system which begins on p. 75. Look at paragraphs 6–8 in it. The relationship between them is very clear, isn't it?

But such numbering can become rather boring, especially for intelligent readers. Look at paragraphs 2–3 in the same essay. They also clearly stand in a first–second relationship, but the writer didn't use *second*. Instead, the first sentence of paragraph 3 uses "also" to make clear that a new point is being introduced. The ability to use this kind of disguised numbering is one mark of a good writer, and the ability to recognize it is one mark of a good reader. Look at example (35), about credit cards, which begins on p. 68. Can you find any numbering in it?

2. Changing Direction

One common reason why writers begin new paragraphs is that they want to present a contrasting idea. In such cases, the first sentence of the new paragraph often contains a word or expression like *however, although,* or *on the other hand.* Here are two examples:

VI. From the Paragraph to the Whole Essay

(a)   At the office, my sister is thought to be an ideal colleague. She is organized, communicative, and considerate. She does her work carefully and is often praised for her contributions to the section.

   At home, <u>however</u>, . . .

(b)   The residents have become quite annoyed by crows. Because of the ugly-voiced black birds, visits to neighborhood parks are not as pleasant as they used to be. Small songbirds have been driven away. Worst of all is the crows' love of garbage. In parks, they take trash from trash cans and spread it everywhere. In residential areas, the crows not only attack and rip open plastic garbage bags, but also find ways to knock over and open garbage cans. Many people are begging the local government to do something to control them.

   Environmentalists, <u>on the other hand</u>, . . .

In (a), the first paragraph says many nice things about the writer's sister. Do you think the writer is going to continue to say pleasant things about her sister in the second paragraph? How about (b)? The idea of the first paragraph is perhaps that the residents would like the crows to be killed or driven away. What idea do you expect to be presented in the second paragraph?

A change in direction may be indicated in other ways, too. How are changes shown in the following sentences?

> This dream was not to come true.
> My father had a very different opinion.
> The results were unexpected.

3. Other Connecting Expressions

Most of the types of connecting expressions which were mentioned on pp. 57–58 can also be used to link paragraphs. Here are some of the most useful ones:

- (a) moreover, besides, furthermore
- (b) however, although, on the other hand, instead, on the contrary
- (c) for example, for instance
- (d) therefore, consequently, thus, on account of this, accordingly
- (e) next, after that, at the same time, then, at this moment [point], first, in the first place, finally, meanwhile, from now on, later
- (f) likewise, similarly, more (troublesome), less (useful), an even better [worse] (idea)
- (g) to sum up, in conclusion

EXERCISE 1. <*Suggested Writing*> Look once more at the information given about the condominium on p. 66. Pretend that you are studying marketing. Your teacher has told you to write an analysis of why apartments in Utsukushiki Mansion are selling so well. Write a five-paragraph essay.

EXERCISE 2. <Suggested Writing> Look back at the paragraphs in the earlier part of this book. Find one with a topic that interests you and try to change it into a longer composition. You can use the ideas in the original, if you like, or add others of your own.

EXERCISE 3. Read the following example. Find the thesis statement. Can you find topic sentences for most of the paragraphs? Are there any transitional paragraphs? Then answer the remaining questions at the end.

The Cost of the *Tanshin-Funin* System

[1]American companies are similar to Japanese companies in that they sometimes need to transfer employees from one city or one country to another, and this is one reason that we hear so much about American mobility. Families sell their homes and move somewhere else. But in Japan, it is very common to hear about *tanshin-funin* (going to a new area to take up a post without one's family). There are a large number of employees who do not live with their spouses and children because they have been assigned to a job in a distant city. This odd system is very harmful.

[2]First of all, it is far more costly to live apart than to live together. Maintaining a home in one city and an apartment in another means paying a great deal of extra rent. The family will also have to pay utility bills for both residences and perhaps need to own two cars. Furthermore, since they will try to see each other as often as possible, they run up expensive travel bills, too.

[3]There is also a great human cost. The parent living away not only loses emotional support from the family, but also needs to be

solely responsible for all the household chores—cooking, cleaning, doing laundry, and so on—on top of working a full-time job. Back at home, the other spouse, who also may have a full-time job, also has more stress, needing to raise the children, make necessary daily decisions, and deal with the normal problems of life more or less as a single parent. The children will grow up knowing one parent much better than the other and may come to feel that the *tanshin-funin* parent is a stranger.

⁴Why is this necessary? Why don't entire families move together if one parent is transferred?

⁵Although the choice is a hard one, there are some good reasons why a parent might decide to move alone. My own father lived separately from us for seven years when I was a child. We had moved with him several times, but he decided to transfer without us after my brother entered junior high school. The reasons for his decision were his own mobility, anxiety about our adaptability to the new environment, and concern about our education.

⁶First, since he worked for a company that had branches in many cities in Japan and often transferred men in their thirties and forties, he could not avoid being ordered to move every few years. Refusal could have reduced his chances to get ahead in the company. All of us were forced to lead an unstable life, because we did not know when he would be transferred. Then, whenever he received a new appointment and moved with us, he had a lot of worries, not only in the office but also at home. Of course he had to get used to his new job, and this required a great deal of care. At the same time, he had to find a new house for our family of four, prepare and send notices of our change of address, and report our change of schools at the city office. Although my

mother helped him, his time was occupied with these things. But if he moved alone, he could move readily and concentrate on his work.

⁷Second, the social organization in Japan tends to be exclusive, and a newcomer has to take great pains to blend in with it. After we moved to a new place, we always had a hard time getting adapted to our new environment. We were tired mentally as well as physically. For a while, wherever we went, we suffered from the strain of getting used to new things. My father could not bear to see our suffering, and he hesitated to make us move any more.

⁸The third, and the most difficult, problem for Japanese families that move is the education of children. As children grow older, it gets harder for them to change schools. One reason is that a transfer student will spend a great deal of time getting accustomed to a new school. The other reason is that changing schools is a disadvantage in getting ready for an entrance examination. Parents consider children's mental stress and the differences in the level of study from one school to another, and hesitate to have the children transfer. It is particularly hard for high school students to change schools, for they are not permitted to enter a new school unless it has a vacancy.

⁹My father's decision to take up his new posts alone did bring some advantages to my family. He could devote himself to his work, and we children had a stable physical and educational environment. But these advantages could not make us forget the burdens, financial and especially emotional, of living apart.

¹⁰Moving together and living together as a family unit, as American families would normally do, is much better than what my family endured. But we would have been even happier if Jap-

anese custom had allowed my father to refuse frequent transfers without penalty, or to change jobs. The *tanshin-funin* system is too hard on human beings. It violates basic human rights!

———Adapted from a student composition

a. Is there anything in the concluding paragraph that reminds you of the introductory paragraph?

b. Has the writer repeated the idea of her thesis statement again in the last paragraph? Has she used the same words?

c. Are there any words or phrases in the final paragraph that make you sense the strength of the writer's feelings?

d. Do paragraphs 2–9 all support the idea that the system is harmful? Why might this be so?

EXERCISE 4. Here are two essays which follow fairly simple patterns. Read them, label the important parts, and draw lines under all the words and expressions which help connect the different paragraphs.

a. Supermarkets and the Environment

¹We often think it wasteful to see the excess of packaging and the plastic shopping bags we get when we go to a supermarket. The stores provide these things as a service, but people who care about the environment tend to criticize the supermarkets. How can the stores force us to end up with so much trash? Don't

they know that Japanese national resources are limited?

²On investigation, however, I found that almost all big supermarkets are grappling with the ecological problems caused by their packaging and their bags. They are trying three kinds of measures: encouraging customers not to use plastic bags, reducing the number of styrofoam trays they use, and recycling such trays, milk cartons, and empty cans and bottles.

³Almost all big supermarkets have adopted a system under which they charge the customer for a plastic bag. These supermarkets also sell original eco-shopping bags which customers can use again and again. But as there are still customers who use the plastic bags for garbage bags or who cannot bring their own shopping bags because they go to the supermarket on their way home from work, it is difficult to completely do away with plastic bag use.

⁴The stores seem to be having more success in reducing the number of styrofoam trays they use. Nowadays we often see fruit and vegetables without trays. I remember that such foods were almost always sold on trays and wrapped in plastic wrap until a few years ago. Now, many kinds of produce are either bare or are wrapped directly. But this change has caused some other problems. When I asked the manager of my local supermarket about packaged fruit and vegetables, he had a complaint to make: "If we remove the trays, fruit and vegetables get bruised easily, and then we cannot sell them." It is true that customers buying fresh produce tend to rummage to find the best. We must be careful when we touch fruit and vegetables.

⁵Recycling is the most difficult of the three for stores to carry out since it needs customers' active cooperation. For recycling, the supermarket must collect waste articles such as milk cartons, styrofoam trays, or empty cans and bottles. But customers think it

is a bother to wash them and take them back to the store. So they are likely to neglect their duty. My mother cooperates by collecting milk cartons. Anytime she finds a carton empty, she cuts it open with scissors, washes it, and dries it. After collecting a few of them, she takes them to the supermarket. It certainly is a bother. If customers are not determined to help, recycling efforts will not be very effective.

⁶It is not true, then, that supermarkets are not doing anything for the environment. But they certainly could and should do more, and all of us customers must make a responsible effort to cooperate. ——Adapted from a student composition

b. Work as a Means

¹One of my high school teachers once told me that I should not be a laborer, but a worker. He meant to say that I should do work which I could be proud of. In those days, I agreed with him completely and thought that I would engage in a sophisticated profession of which I could be proud and, at the same time, one which would make other people look up to me. But now I have changed my mind. Of course, it is very desirable for people to love their jobs. But I wonder whether it is good to have pride in one's job. I also doubt that we should look up to someone because of his or her job. I think there are some serious problems that occur when people try to find pride or value in a job.

²The first problem connected with having pride in or attaching special value to one's work is that such an attitude gives rank or social status to work which was originally just a means of earning money. For example, people such as doctors, lawyers, and college professors are regarded as important, excellent, and wor-

thy of other people's respect. None of them offer their services for free. Of course we pay for them. In this respect we are in equal positions. Our mistake is to give up that equality and give them admiration, which is unnecessary.

³What is even worse is that we tend to make connections between certain kinds of work and moral character. Newspapers provide interesting examples of this. We sometimes find articles which say, "The honest taxi driver sent his passenger the money which was left behind in his car," or "The thief was a police officer!" These expressions hint that we are likely to believe that taxi drivers are not so honest and that all police officers must be perfect people. Indeed, we never hear phrases like "the honest police officer" or "the honest teacher." Thus, without realizing it, we judge other people's characters by their jobs, and now and then insult them or overestimate them.

⁴This tendency causes another problem. Because people judge others by their work, it becomes desirable to get jobs which can gain other people's respect and trust for us. Now, what most parents are interested in is to get their children into a respected profession or a respected large company. In order to do so, they make their children study very hard. At home, children must obey tutors, and at private schools, teachers train them rigorously. Is it any wonder that at school or play they are too tired to enjoy themselves? Placing value on certain professions robs children of their childhood.

⁵Thus I think it better to regard jobs as just a means of earning the money we need than to endow jobs with a special value. People should be valued for their characters and personalities, not for the work they do. Work should be a means of earning a living, not a means of labeling people. ——Adapted from a student composition

Essays like a. and b. (pp. 78–81) mainly follow the pattern of

Introduction + 3 supporting paragraphs + conclusion
 = essay

This makes them relatively easy to write and to read. But as we mentioned earlier, of course very few essays follow this simple pattern exactly. In a. above, there is an extra paragraph, and that part of the essay does not fit the 1 + 3 + 1 pattern. Where is the introductory paragraph? Where is the thesis statement?

C. For Further Thought

The following essays may seem even further from the 1 + 3 + 1 pattern. Try to analyze them. Where is the thesis statement? How is the main idea supported?

(36) The Importance of Words

On Wednesday on the way to school, I felt depressed. Nothing was going well. For weeks I had been so busy with my club and my part-time job that I had not been able to sleep very much. I had not prepared well for that day's classes. I had not made any progress in writing my assignment because I could not use the fingers on my left hand very well. I had not cleaned my room for a long time, and there was a horrible pile of dirty clothes that got higher every day. I was thinking how inefficient I was.

In front of the gate, I met one of the older students in my club.

"Hello," I said.

"Hello. You look a little gloomy today. Is anything wrong?"

"Well, recently I've had a lot to do, and so I feel rather tired."

"Hmmm. That isn't good. You really do seem to have a tight schedule."

"Yes, I'm afraid I've lost my sense of direction."

"But look on the bright side of things. It proves that you are leading a full life, doesn't it? You usually look so cheerful. I've always admired your smile."

"Really?"

"Yes! Please cheer up and show it to me."

Her words cleared my mind like a bracing wind. She had said she liked my smile! My faltering heart recovered, thanks to her encouraging words. Now I enjoy every day with energy, smiling.

I may be just a simple person. However, I learned that words can have a great effect on us. My words can cheer you up, or, on the other hand, they can hurt you. I should be careful about it so that I can use words skillfully like the club member who spoke to me.   ——Adapted from a student composition

(37) The Importance of Attitude

Today, quitting one's job before really mastering it is very common, especially among young people. I do not think it is completely wrong, because it is not good for people to continue their jobs if they hate the work. However, is there no possibility that they may become interested in that same work only by changing their way of thinking?

Last summer vacation, I worked in an office regularly five

days a week. The company is fairly big, and is divided into lots of sections, probably twenty or thirty. I was sent to one of them like other part-timers.

For the first week, I got tired very easily and wanted to quit. I think it was probably because I did only one kind of operation. For example, on the first day I just calculated and filled out forms from morning till night. On the next day, I called customers. And the next day...and so on. For the first half of each day, I felt interested to find out about the new job, but soon I got weary of it. In addition, I was just following the instructions the manager gave me. I did not know what my work meant or why I was doing it. To follow her instructions step by step was easy, but on the other hand it was very boring. I felt small and useless. Workers at big companies sometimes complain that they are just small cogs in a big machine, and I felt the same way. But whatever the reasons, although I was doing very easy tasks, I got exhausted.

Then one day the manager called me. "You have learned almost all the operations in our section," she said. "Now I'll explain to you about the relationship between them and their purpose. When we get papers from Section A, first we circle the proper blank with a red pen. I think you did that on Tuesday, didn't you?"

"Yes," I said. ("Very boring task!" I thought.)

"Then we call customers to get information. Have you done that?"

"Yes, I did it once," I answered. (And hated it.)

She explained various things like that. I was surprised to find that all the small tasks I had done had some connection with each other, and that as a result of my work the company had done a lot of business. I was moved by the fact that I was doing something useful for the company after all, and felt myself a real part of it. After that I got interested in my job, in spite of doing exactly the same work as before. I became more alert and involved as I worked, because now I knew what the important point of each operation was.

 Our attitude toward the job is very important. If we constantly think about why we are doing each part of our job, if we consider both the big and the small aims of each task, we may realize that what we are doing is important and come to care about doing it well. If people could look at their jobs again from various points of view, I think most of them would not quit so easily. ——Adapted from a student composition

Probably you realized that in essay (36) there is no introductory paragraph which explains the writer's purpose. The title gives us a hint as to the thesis statement, which the writer supports with one convincing example and then explains directly in the concluding paragraph.

 Incidentally, this essay also provides a good chance to observe how dialogue is written. First, each time the speaker changes, the writer starts a new paragraph. Second, the writer uses "I said" only once. Since there are only two speakers, and it is clear which one is which, it is unnecessary to repeat "I said" and "she said" every time. For readers, it would also be annoying to see "I said" or "she said" too often.

 In the essay about attitude, you probably saw that the writer has presented her central idea in the first and last paragraphs. Everything in between is a single personal example which makes that idea both clearer and more interesting.

By this time, you know a lot about English writing. But the secret to actually becoming a good writer is to read and write as much as possible. Good luck!

VI. From the Paragraph to the Whole Essay

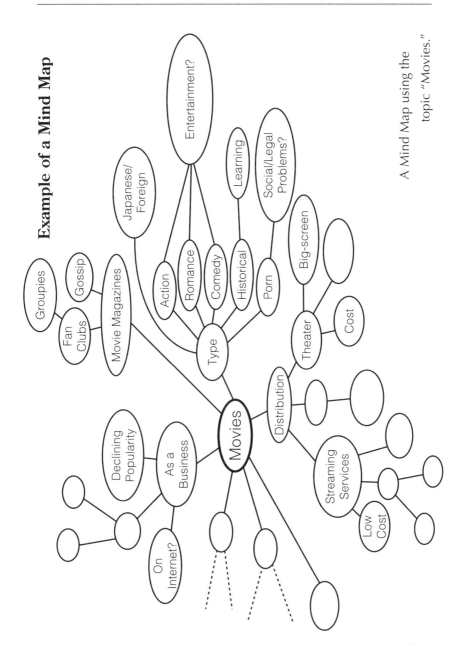

A Mind Map using the topic "Movies."

A Brief Guide to American Punctuation

Below you will find examples of various kinds of punctuation which are often needed in English writing at the university level. The rules which go with many of the examples have been omitted, on the grounds that examples are often easier to understand than rules. If you do not understand the usage in a particular example, ask your teacher or consult a full-length punctuation manual.

The Period
    I am a college student.
    The plane leaves at 6 a.m. （文の最後の period は 1 つ）

The Question Mark
    How can we learn to use time wisely?

The Exclamation Point
    I can't believe my eyes!
    You fool!
    Come back!

The Semicolon
    The sun went down; the day slowly drew to a close.
    Lincoln was reelected in 1864; however, he was assassinated less than a year later.

Punctuation helps readers; therefore, writers should pay more attention to it. （semicolon の後には接続詞は不要．however, therefore は接続副詞）

The Colon

For many years there were only three big networks in the United States: ABC, CBS, and NBC. （例などのリスト）

The book was badly planned: there was no coherent theme and many necessary topics had been left out. （説明）

Dear Dr. Smith: （手紙の書き出し〈formal な場合〉）

The train is scheduled to leave at 3:15. （時刻）

The White Plum: A Biography of Ume Tsuda （副題）

Ume expressed her feelings in the following way: "My heart goes out to Japanese women, and I burn with indignation at their position, while I blame them too." （引用〈完結した節により導入される場合〉）

The Comma

I ordered pancakes, bacon, and coffee.

Haruka listens to music while she's eating, while she's commuting, and while she's studying. （3つ以上の語句を並べる場合，and の前にもつけることが望ましい）

The owner was a tall, red-haired woman.

The tall, athletic American teacher is Ms. Whittaker. （同じ類のいくつかの形容詞を並べる場合）

The first American president was George Washington, a general in the Revolutionary War.

George Washington, the first American President, was a general in the Revolutionary War. （同格の語句の前後）

We Japanese sometimes have a hard time saying no. （We Japanese のように両者で一体感のある場合には comma をつけない）

I'm sorry that you misunderstood me, Emi.

I'm sorry, Emi, that you misunderstood me.

Of course, there are many people who would not agree with my analysis.

He was told, nevertheless, that he could get a loan.

Oh, surely you don't mean that!　（呼び掛けの語句，感嘆詞など，文の途中にさしはさむ語句）

Fearing that the burglar might return, I locked all the windows carefully.

When he came back from his vacation in Europe, he found that his car had been stolen.

Shohei Ohtani, who excels at both pitching and batting, is often compared to Babe Ruth.

The sunglasses, which are on sale, are in that cabinet. (Readers will understand that all the sunglasses are on sale and that all the sunglasses are in the cabinet.)

The sunglasses which are on sale are in that cabinet. (Readers will understand that there are also some sunglasses which are not on sale and which are not in the cabinet.)

The park's monkeys, which are not dangerous, are allowed to wander around freely. (Readers will understand that none of the monkeys is dangerous.)

The park's monkeys which are not dangerous are allowed to wander around freely. (Readers will assume that there are also some dangerous monkeys which are not allowed to wander around freely.)

（制限的用法と非制限的用法〈comma をつける〉の区別に注意）

Someone had left the door open, and a strange cat walked confidently into our living room.

He badly wanted to go to college, but his parents did not believe in the value of education.　（重文では節の終わりに）

She grew up in a house located at 524 Ingham Avenue, Columbus, Ohio.

Send your applications to TJ College, 2–1–1 Minami-machi, Kokubunji-shi, Tokyo 185–0043.　（住所）

He graduated from college on March 18, 2019.

 cf. He graduated from college in March 2019.　（日付）

Emily P. Gruber, M.D.　(M.D. = Doctor of Medicine)

Pauline Samson, Professor of Law

Merkel, Angela Dorothea

Clinton, William Jefferson

Gore, Albert, Jr.

Gruber, Emily P., M.D.　（姓，名の順の時，および肩書）

Confusing:　Just when I was about to get off the bus hit a truck.

Clear:　Just when I was about to get off, the bus hit a truck.

（comma がないと間違いやすい場合）

Quotation Marks

"I'll call you as soon as I get home," she promised Drew.

We all wondered what had happened. I asked, "Did he say, 'I'll call you as soon as I get home,' or 'I'll call you soon'?"

Everyone tried to comfort Tatum. Riley said soothingly, "Look, Tatum, there's no sense in crying over someone who says, 'I never want to see you again.'"　（引用では comma と引用符の位置に注意．引用の中にさらに引用が入る場合は " ' " となる）

Everything in your composition marked "ww" (for "wrong word") should be changed to a better vocabulary word.

In the last sentence of your composition, "I think" sounds too weak.　（語句をそのまま文中に入れる場合）

In what year did Martin Luther King, Jr., give his "I Have a Dream" speech?

Aretha Franklin's version of "Bridge over Troubled Water" is one of my favorite songs.

"A Haunted House" is a short story written by Virginia Woolf. （スピーチ，歌，短編小説の題など）

Direct Quotations

"I hate carrots," the boy screamed.

The president said, "Well, that is a possibility."

"I think," she said, "that you had better leave."

"Who is going to pay for this?" he asked.

He asked, "Who is going to pay for this?"

"Put that gun down!" I cried.

I cried, "Put that gun down!"

Who said, "We have nothing to fear but fear itself"?

Believe it or not, but after fifteen years in prison he said, "I have come to enjoy life behind bars"!　（文の最後の句読点の位置に注意．主節が疑問文，主節の話し手が感嘆詞をつけたい場合など）

Ellipsis

The explanation of ellipsis in the textbook says, "When words are omitted from . . . a quotation, a series of three periods is used to show the omission."　（引用文の中の省略は period を3つつけ，間隔をあける．文の最後では，さらに必要な period などの句読点が加わる）

The Hyphen

I employed a fifteen-year-old boy to help me in my yard.

Use an up-to-date dictionary.　（名詞の前に置く形容詞の複合語句に hyphen が必要）

cf. Use a dictionary which is up to date.

The Dash
I got a pair of ice skates—and a fine pair of skates they were—for Christmas.

My sister-in-law—my older brother's wife—is in the hospital to have a baby. （dash は hyphen 2つ分の長さで，前後にスペースを入れない）

The Apostrophe
I was surprised to see my friend's mother.

Everyone looked for John's book.

We were all shocked by the news of the princess's death.

During the holidays I enjoyed visiting my friends' homes.
（名詞が複数形であって，かつ綴りが s で終わる場合，所有格には apostrophe のみを用いる）

Mother Goose is a famous children's book.

My sister attends a women's college.

My wife and I live in my mother-in-law's house.

Here is an old photo of the Prince of Wales's family.

This is no one else's business.

The problem had little effect on the University of Kyoto's reputation.

We had a long discussion about Biden and Harris's environmental policy. （2人以上の人が共有する場合）

She is analyzing Hillary Clinton's and Barack Obama's campaign speeches. （それぞれ別のスピーチの場合）

I don't have enough time to do it now.

It's (= It is) almost noon.
   cf. How often does the snake shed its skin?

Parentheses
> During World War II (1941–45), women made great inroads into American industry.
>
> I have had my faithful MacBook (I would never own any other kind of laptop!) for three years now.
>
> A five-paragraph essay consists of (a) an introductory paragraph, (b) three paragraphs in the body of the essay, and (c) a concluding paragraph.

The Slash
> Greta Gerwig is the writer/director of *Lady Bird*, which was nominated for five Oscars at the 90th Academy Awards.

Italics
> You should use italics only to show *strong* emphasis.
> （語句をとくに強調したい時）
>
> Beginning practitioners of *iaido*, the martial art of drawing a Japanese sword, sometimes use a wooden sword. (Japanese)
>
> The French expression *quel dommage* means "What a pity!" (French)
>
> We changed the tatami mats in our house at the end of December. (Japanese)
> （英語以外の言語の語句を文中で使う時．ただしその語句が *Merriam-Webster's Collegiate Dictionary* のような標準的な辞典に掲載されている場合，italics は用いない）
>
> The word *color* has a different spelling in British English. （語句そのものをそのまま文中で使う時）
>
> *The Japan Times*
> *Pride and Prejudice*

La La Land
Hamlet
Newsweek
　（新聞，単行本，映画，劇，雑誌名）

Acknowledgments

From *On Writing the Short Story* by Hallie S. Burnett. Copyright ©1983 Reprinted with permission from HarperCollins Publishers, Inc.

Reproduced from *THE MIDDLE GROUND* by Dame Margaret Drabble CBE (Copyright © Margaret Drabble, 1980) by permission of United Agents Ltd (www.unitedagents.co.uk) on behalf of Dame Margaret Drabble CBE.

Cross Section からの転載許諾: 株式会社構造システム

KENKYUSHA

〈検印省略〉

Effective Writing: From the Paragraph Up
(New Revised Edition)
パラグラフから始める英文ライティング入門(新訂版)

2024 年 11 月 29 日　初版発行

編著者　津田塾大学英語英文学科
発行者　吉田　尚志
印刷所　TOPPAN クロレ株式会社

発行所　株式会社　研究社

〒102-8152
東京都千代田区富士見 2-11-3
電話 (編集) 03 (3288) 7711 (代)
　　 (営業) 03 (3288) 7777 (代)
振替 00150-9-26710
https://www.kenkyusha.co.jp/

ISBN978-4-327-42204-2　C3082　　Printed in Japan
装丁　株式会社明昌堂

価格はカバーに表示してあります。
本書のコピー、スキャン、デジタル化等の無断複製は、著作権上の例外を除き、禁じられています。私的使用以外のいかなる電子的複製行為も一切認められていません。乱丁本、落丁本はお取替えいたします。ただし、中古品についてはお取替えできません。